STUDY

# WHEN SKIES AREN'T BLUE

*A Physician's Personal Journey*

ANDY LAURIE, MD

*with Nicole Baron*

*When Skies Aren't Blue Study Guide: A Physician's Personal Journey*



The scripture verses used in *When Skies Aren't Blue* are from the New American Standard Bible (NASB).

Published by Andy Laurie, MD
Cover and book design by Nicole Baron Designs

ISBN: 978-1-7364139-2-0
LCCN: 2023924536

# CONTENTS

# HOW TO USE THIS GUIDE

**INDIVIDUAL OR GROUP STUDY:** This guide has been designed for either group or individual study. Regardless of which approach you choose, please complete each section, taking the time to fill in all the blanks and to write down your answers to each of the discussion questions. The discussion questions and blanks are a vital part of each lesson and are designed to augment the learning experience.

**FACILITATOR:** Should you choose a group study, each group should appoint a facilitator. Facilitators should open with prayer, read through each section—including author's notes—*out loud* (or ask others to do so) and guide the discussions, prompting participants to respond and ensure that everyone has an opportunity to participate. **BEFORE YOU BEGIN:** Make sure to review the leader's notes located at the end of each section that provide answers to the blanks and pertinent guidance for the discussion questions. We recommend that you use these notes to fill in the blanks in your copy of the study guide ahead of time before the group meets. This will help the group run smoother as you lead them through the discussion.

**MATERIALS NEEDED:** Each participant will need their own copy of this study guide, a Bible and a pencil/pen. All Bible verses used in this study are from the New American Standard Version unless otherwise indicated. While this study guide stands on its own, we encourage each participant to have their own copy of the book, *When Skies Aren't Blue.* Reading the corresponding section in *When Skies Aren't Blue* prior to each lesson will greatly enhance the learning experience.

**DR. ANDY'S TREATMENT PLAN:** Each section ends with a helpful "treatment plan" for you. We want this guide to be hands-on and practical. Please put those treatment plans into action in your life. You will be surprised at how the power of God will work through them to brighten even the darkest of skies.

So, let's begin our journey to blue skies together.

STEP 1

# *We Need A Hope That Is Real*

*The starting point of healing when our skies turn dark is understanding that our God is very real.*

# GROUP DISCUSSION

**START HERE** Welcome to Step 1 of our study guide; let's begin with prayer (you can use the one below as a guide).

*Father, please use this lesson to help us develop a confident faith. Help us to know that You are real, and Your promises are true. And that You will work for good in whatever may be darkening our skies. In Jesus name, Amen.*

Author's Note

*If any discussion questions in this guide are too personal for you to share in the group setting, you do not need to discuss them openly, but make sure to write them down. This way, you can go back and apply the principles you learn through this study to those specific struggles that are darkening the skies of your life.*

(Answers to blanks found on page 10.)

**1** The skies in my life rapidly turned dark following an ongoing, debilitating chronic illness. But my story is not unique. As a physician and pastor, I have seen many people over the years whose skies have been darkened by different struggles. Failing health is just one struggle that we face.

***What are some of the most common struggles that darken the skies in the lives of people around you?***

***Now let's make this a bit more personal. What about you? What is darkening the skies in your life?***

2 I have seen both in my own life and in others' that these dark sky times can so easily tear away our faith.

***Why do you think these difficult times can erode our spiritual foundation? Come up with your own list below.***

## AUTHOR'S LIST

- Our faith is ________________, not built on the right foundation to withstand these storms.
- We tend to blame _____________ for our suffering, which further erodes our trust relationship with Him.
- We have ____________ ______________________ of how our lives should go in this world, leading to resentment and bitterness.
- Many of these struggles, especially the ones with physical and mental health problems, tend to _____________ our thinking process. This can undermine our ability to navigate our way back to brighter skies.
- We have not strengthened ourselves mentally or spiritually ahead of time. So, we are ______________________ when these struggles hit.
- The struggles can paralyze us from taking the _____________ we need to find blue skies.

- When the struggles become ongoing, our sadness over the life we have lost can prevent us from moving ________________ in a new life.
- The struggle causes us to become so focused on the ______________, that we fail to step back and see the big picture. We fail to see how God is ___________ ____________________ in our lives.
- Our thought process can become so consumed with the negative that all we see are ______________ ___________.
- We can begin to think that our lives will always be this dark struggle, as we lose sight of our ______________ ___________.

Author's Note

*We will address each one of these and so much more through the course of this study. But these are many of the reasons that dark sky struggles can so easily erode our spiritual foundation.*

*If you put God's biblical principles in place (that you will learn in this study), you will have that powerful spiritual foundation that God can and will use to brighten even the darkest of skies. So, let's go.*

3

Now you might be thinking, *"Is there something spiritually wrong with me? Why is this dark sky time causing such a challenge for my faith?"* No, there is nothing wrong with you. Even the most faithful of us will face that challenge. I want you to consider one of the greatest men of faith in the Bible: John the Baptist. Let's see what happened to the faith of this man of God (read Matthew 11:2-3).

***So, what happened to the faith of John?***

John ______________ Jesus. He told his followers to go ask Jesus, "Are you the Expected One, or shall we look for someone else?"

4 So, John doubted. John's whole life was dedicated to pointing people to the Expected One—Jesus. And now, he is questioning if Jesus is in fact the Expected One. Think about everything he saw and heard (including the Spirit of God coming upon Jesus when John baptized Him). And yet *now*, John is doubting?

***Why do you think John is having this crisis of faith and now doubting Jesus?***

John was now doubting because he was facing some very ________ __________. John was in prison for standing for God. He knew he was going to be executed—very dark skies indeed. And in the midst of those dark skies—this great man of faith—doubted! Dark skies have a way of doing that to all of us.

5 John, in this dark sky time, sends his messengers to Jesus relaying this "doubt", asking Jesus, "Are you the Expected One?" Jesus' response is fascinating (read Matthew 11:4-5).

***What does Jesus tell John that he needs to be focusing on to combat this doubt?***

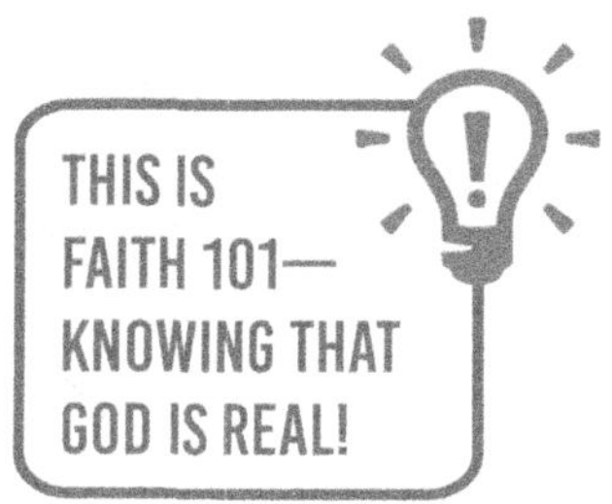


Jesus tells John's followers to go back and remind John of ________ ______________. He points to ______________ that were *heard* and *seen*. The specific miracles Jesus mentioned were __________________ found in the Old Testament that the future Messiah would perform. Jesus knew that John would be familiar with those. This is fascinating! The God who knows us inside and out is showing us that when we face those dark skies, we need those facts. This is faith 101—knowing that God is real!

6

"God never intended for us to believe on blind faith because He knew when our skies turned dark, we would need the confidence."

*When Skies Aren't Blue,* page 22

Let's look at the concept of "blind faith" as it relates to dark sky times. Atheists—to ridicule Christians—will define "blind faith" as: believing in *the absence of evidence.* Not surprising, God tells us something very different. He tells us about the power of evidence-based faith. God knows that faith without _______________ will fall short on many levels.

***What type of struggles in our lives would be particularly difficult to cope with if our faith was without evidence (blind faith)?***

## AUTHOR'S LIST

- If you are in a ________________ ________________ and everything, including your survival, is on the line, it won't work to just kind of hope God is there—you need to know.
- If you are in a ___________________ ________________ you need to know that God's promises are true. And He will work out those financial details for those who truly put Him first.
- How about when we face our __________ ____________________? We need to know (not hope or wish) that heaven is a very real place for those who have chosen to get right and live right for Christ.

Regardless of what the struggle may be, there are those dark sky moments where we need to *know* God is real, God is true and God's got our back. He always has and always will. And that is why having that solid *evidence* is so critical.

VICIOUS CIRCLE

VICIOUS CIRCLE BROKEN

The graphic above illustrates how destructive dark sky times can be to our faith. Life will inevitably smack us down with one of those awful struggles that darken our skies. And that can cause even the best of us to doubt God. Doubting God in turn weakens our faith, further darkening our skies. It is indeed a ________________ ____________.

***What do you think is the key to breaking that vicious circle?***

Getting the facts which prove God, Jesus and the Bible must be _________ is the key to breaking that vicious circle.

Author's Note

*You might be wondering, "Where can I find these facts?" There are many sources available on the web. In addition, there are some classic books I pointed out in* When Skies Aren't Blue *by Josh McDowell and Lee Stroebel. But one of my favorite sources, especially for those who are visual learners, is a seminar by The Bridge Christian Church called "Facts Behind The Faith." Just a few hours viewing this seminar will provide a powerful foundation to overcome the doubt brought on by even the darkest of skies. You can find a link to that free seminar on my web page: whenskiesarentblue.com.*

**8** In addition to these facts, there is something else that is critical to developing a rock-solid faith in God (read Romans 1:20).

***Where does this verse say we should also look to find proof for the reality of God?***

This verse is teaching us to look at ______________ as a source of proof for God.

Based on this verse, I have a mental exercise I like to do, especially when this lousy disease challenges my faith. As a physician, I know the human body is a ____________________ of incredible complexity. Our minds cannot begin to comprehend the level of sophistication of this human machine. And we know that every machine must have a ____________________. Based on this—here is my mental exercise:

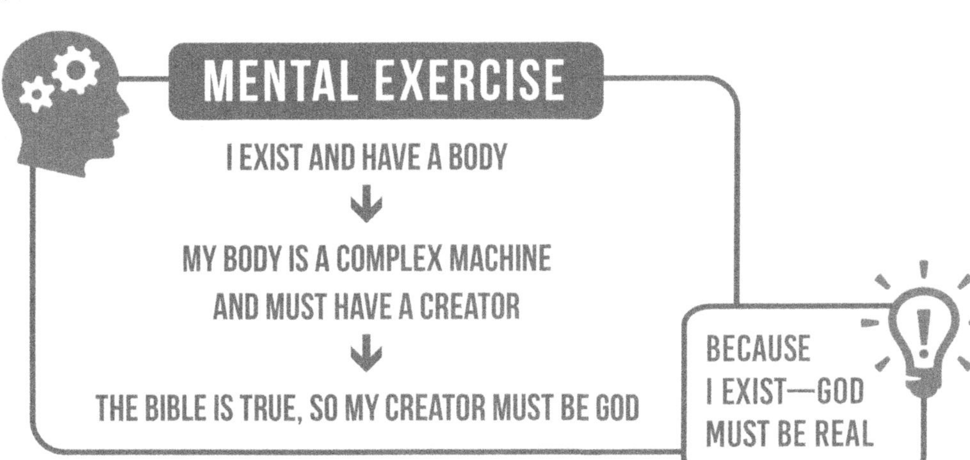


Author's Note

*If you have questions about how this plays out with the failed theory of Darwinian Macroevolution, please check out a very helpful seminar by The Bridge Christian Church, "Creation vs. Evolution." You can find a link to that free seminar on my web page: whenskiesarentblue.com.*

So, whether it is the marvels of the human machine, the birth of a child, a glorious sunset, a stunning waterfall, crashing waves of the ocean or a beautiful rainbow—if we simply look at the majesty of creation with an open heart and objective eyes—it screams of a magnificent Creator—Jesus.

9 One of my favorite verses that describes a *real* and *powerful* faith is found in Hebrews 11:1, which says, "Now faith is the assurance of things hoped for, the conviction of things not seen."

***How can this Hebrews 11:1 faith help you with your struggles?***

God is teaching us that a powerful faith is being *sure* of the things we __________ __________________ so that we can be confident about the things we __________________ __________________.

Because we can prove the Bible is true (the __________________ of things hoped for), we can have confidence that our God is fighting for us behind the scenes (the conviction of things _________ ______________).

That is the kind of powerful faith we will need to gain those blue skies in the midst of the ongoing struggles in this broken world.

10 There is another powerful verse that describes a promise from God in dark sky times (read Romans 8:28).

***How can it bring you comfort and confidence knowing that Romans 8:28 is a factual statement?***

God says, *"I understand that this is a broken world, and your skies are dark. But you can know for a fact that I am real. You just love and obey Me (called according to My purpose). And I will take your struggle and work that together for good. I am real, I've got this and I've got you—I always have and always will."*

Now that is real faith!

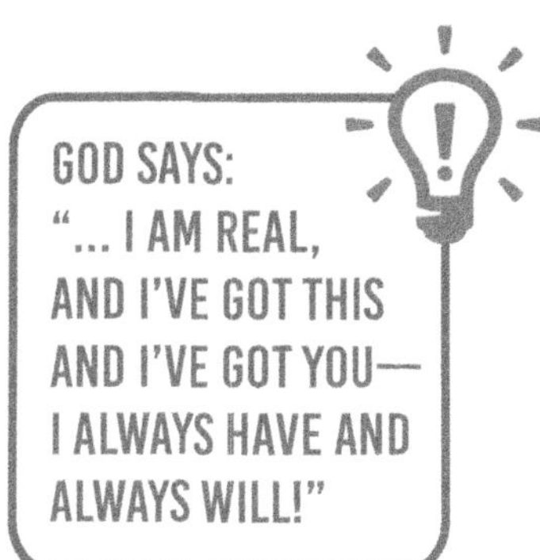


**PROCEED WITH READING DR. ANDY'S TREATMENT PLAN ON PAGE 11.**

# LEADER'S NOTES

1. Possible Answers: Health Struggles (physical and mental), Illness of a loved one (physical and mental), Bereavement (mourning the loss of a loved one), Divorce (failed relationships), Job worries/pressure, Financial Struggles, Broken family relationships, Worries about children's future, Addictions (substance and behavioral) and more.

   Personal Answers. *Allow the group time to write their answers down, sharing is optional.*
2. Blanks: shallow, God, false expectations, cloud, unprepared, action, forward, problem, still working, dark skies, final home
3. Blank: doubted
4. Blanks: dark skies
5. Blanks: the facts, miracles, prophecies
6. Blanks: evidence, health crisis, financial crisis, own mortality
7. Blanks: vicious circle, true
8. Blanks: creation, machine, Creator
9. Blanks: can prove, cannot prove, assurance, not seen
10. Personal Answers. *Allow the group time to write their answers down, sharing is optional if it is too personal.*

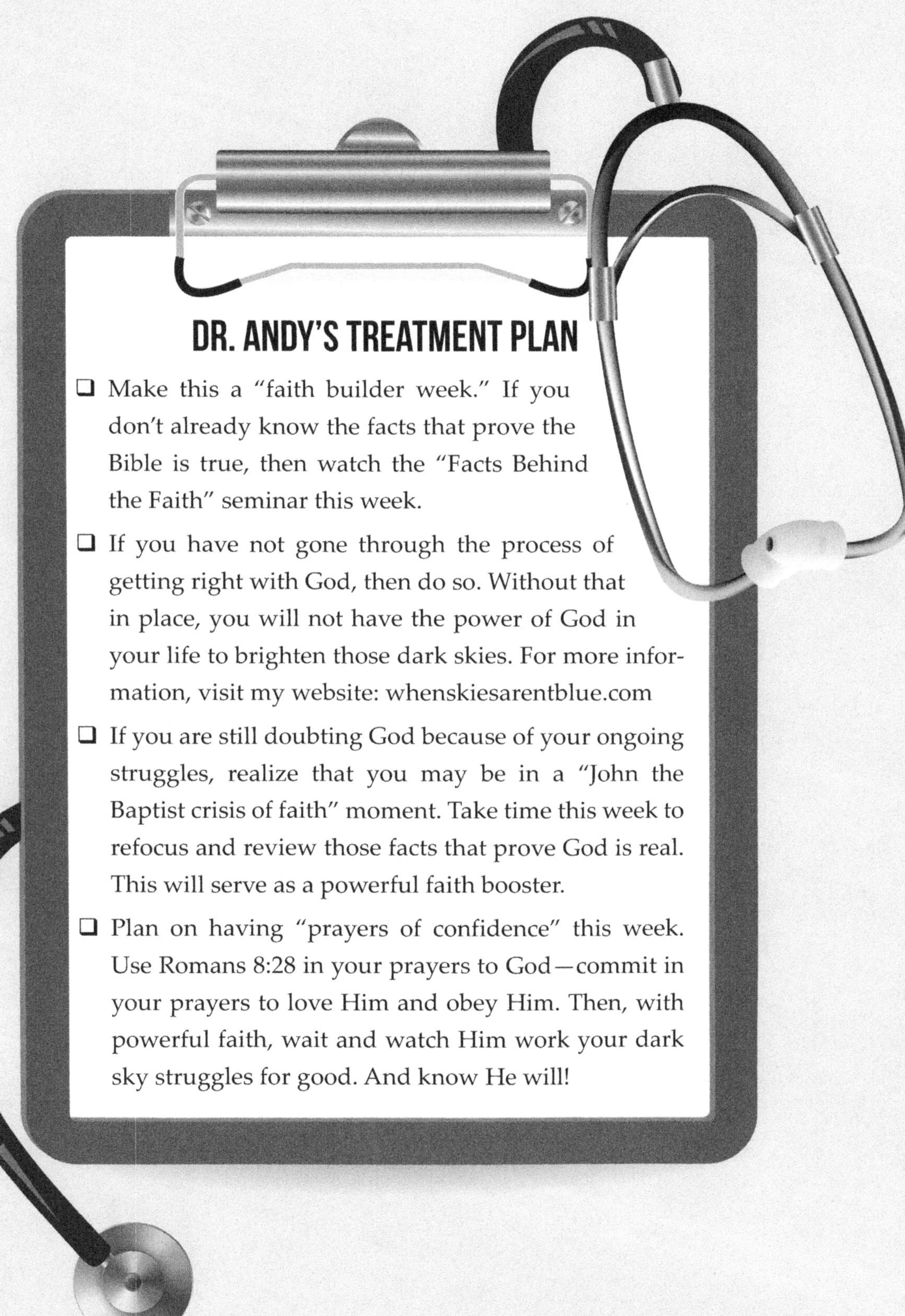

## DR. ANDY'S TREATMENT PLAN

- ❑ Make this a "faith builder week." If you don't already know the facts that prove the Bible is true, then watch the "Facts Behind the Faith" seminar this week.
- ❑ If you have not gone through the process of getting right with God, then do so. Without that in place, you will not have the power of God in your life to brighten those dark skies. For more information, visit my website: whenskiesarentblue.com
- ❑ If you are still doubting God because of your ongoing struggles, realize that you may be in a "John the Baptist crisis of faith" moment. Take time this week to refocus and review those facts that prove God is real. This will serve as a powerful faith booster.
- ❑ Plan on having "prayers of confidence" this week. Use Romans 8:28 in your prayers to God—commit in your prayers to love Him and obey Him. Then, with powerful faith, wait and watch Him work your dark sky struggles for good. And know He will!

STEP 2

# *Know Who Darkened It*

*How could I turn to God for His comfort if deep down I believe that He is the One doing this to me?*

# GROUP DISCUSSION

**START HERE** Congratulations on completing Step 1! We now move on to Step 2: Know Who Darkened It. Let's begin with prayer (you can use the one below as a guide).

*Father, there is so much suffering and hurt in this world and in our lives. I ask that You give us wisdom in this study so that we may understand where this suffering ultimately comes from. Help us to know who the perpetrator of these dark skies is, and who truly is the hero. In Jesus name, Amen.*

**Author's Note**

*As we proceed through this study together, you will see and feel that power of God which can brighten even the darkest skies. You will get a sense for how hard God is fighting for you in your struggles. But I can assure you, all of that will come to a screeching halt if we are holding onto a belief that God is responsible for our suffering. But, if God is not responsible for our suffering, then who or what is? Let's dig in and figure it out.*

(Answers to blanks found on page 22.)

**1** We need to first distinguish between suffering brought on by bad or sinful choices and suffering brought on by no fault of our own. This is a very important concept and needs to be clearly understood.

***In your mind, envision the "perfect Dad". Ask yourself, when he sees that his kids are making dangerous and harmful choices, how should that "perfect Dad" respond?***

***Read Hebrews 12:4-11. Based on this passage, how does our "perfect Dad" respond to His kids when they are making those dangerous choices in life?***

Our Heavenly Dad is going to ___________________ His kids out of _________. He is *not punishing* them for doing wrong, but rather disciplining to help them make right choices. That is what a great Dad does for His kids. In fact, that passage said, if we don't have that discipline in our lives, then we are "illegitimate" and not really His kids. God's discipline is that big of a deal.

2

When it comes to God's discipline, we need to ask ourselves a very important question:

***How can we know if the dark skies in our lives are a result of God's discipline?***

There is a _______________ and _______________ between wrong actions (sin) and the consequences of such choices (read Numbers 32:23). If we are involved in consistent sin and are suffering the dark skies because of it; then yes, it is our Heavenly Father, out of __________, who is bringing this discipline.

***So, if we find ourselves being disciplined by God and facing those dark skies, what should we do?***

We _____________. Repenting is having that heartfelt sorrow for our sin. And that sorrow leads us to change our actions and turn away from that sinful behavior. I know that repenting is not a popular concept in our culture today. But without it, God's discipline will ___________________, and those skies will remain dark.

But here is the wonderful thing: when we choose to repent, our amazing Heavenly Father will be right there for us. And together, you and He will walk through that process of applying what you learn through this study to brighten those dark skies once again.

3

What about the dark skies that come from the struggles and tragedies that are ________ ________________ of our own? We are not making poor/sinful choices and yet we are still hit with this awful suffering. Who or what is to blame for those dark skies? Let's figure this out.

Start with an honest assessment of the world around us. On the one hand, we see much beauty and many wonderful things. But let's face it, there are also so many *tragic* things that define our world.

> ***Come up with a list of tragedies that we see in the world around us that darken so many skies.***

If we were being honest with what we see of the world around us, and the immense suffering that is everywhere, we would admit that our world is very ________________. And a force that is causing this level of pain and suffering would have to be inherently _____________.

**4** Now let's take a look at what the Bible teaches us (read 1 John 5:19, Ephesians 2:2 and Hebrews 2:14).

***Based on these verses, who does the Bible say is responsible for the suffering that we see in this world?***

1 John 5:19: this tells us that the "whole world lies in the power of the ___________ __________." Ephesians 2:2 reveals to us that it is _______________ who is the "prince of the power of the air". Hebrews 2:14 tells us something that is a surprise to many, but it is Satan who, for now, yields the power of _____________.

Scripture teaches us that when sin entered the world in the garden of Eden, this temporary world was placed under a curse and paradise was ___________. Suffering and death are part of that curse and are ____________________ in this broken world.

God certainly has the power to fix every problem in this world. But if He did, it would be ____________________ on earth once again. That time will come ____________________________, when the curse is erased, and it will be eternally amazing. But, for the here and now, we live in this broken world—where the evil power of _______________ darkens our skies.

Author's Note

*Over the years I have had many questions come my way:*

- *If God is not causing these struggles, then isn't He allowing them?*
- *Why can't God just step in and fix all our struggles for us?*
- *If God is in fact all-powerful and sovereign, how can Satan do this?*
- *How long will Satan have this power?*
- *What about the book of Job and how does that pertain to this?*
- *What is going on at a supernatural level to explain all this mess?*
- *Is God still miraculously healing in this broken world?*

*All these questions and much more are clearly answered in a video seminar called "Why Bad Things Happen To Good People". Just go to whenskiesarentblue.com to find the link to that free seminar.*

5 Understanding that God is not the author of suffering in this world is more than just an interesting, intellectual and spiritual discussion. It is in fact vital that we have a healthy grasp on the origins of suffering.

***Come up with at least one reason why it is so critical that we know God is* not *the author of our suffering?***

## AUTHOR'S TOP 4 REASONS

1. It allows us to direct our _______________ towards Satan.
2. Blaming God does not benefit us ______________________.
3. We don't want to give Satan a _______________ _______________.
4. We will not be able to _______________ God.

Let's look at each of these in more detail.

6 **TOP REASON #1** It allows us to direct our anger towards Satan.

Righteous anger is a good thing. If directed appropriately, it can be a __________________ emotion. In part, why I wrote *When Skies Aren't Blue* was to pay back Satan for what he had done to me. I wanted to _______________ him as the evil behind my suffering. Let your righteous anger over what Satan has done to you or a loved one drive you to _______________ for God and to _______________ your world for Christ.

7 **TOP REASON #2** Blaming God does not benefit us emotionally.

I've been sick and suffering for over two decades. I have heard pretty much all the well-intentioned clichés to try and spiritually explain my ongoing illness: *God has a reason. God is teaching you something. Who can know the mind of God?*

But these clichés do not work in the *real* world with *real* suffering. When I am sick to my stomach every single morning, it brings me *no emotional solace* to know that *God has a reason* and wants to *teach me something.* When my life has been destroyed by this illness and my family has suffered through it all, it brings me *no emotional comfort* that *I cannot know the mind of God.*

These clichés all have the same foundational message:

God is the one ______________________ for our suffering. But the problem is that when we suffer, blaming God will devastate us *emotionally*. It will lead to ______________________ towards Him at the deepest level of our soul.

8 **TOP REASON #3** It gives Satan a double victory.

The last thing we want to do is give Satan a double victory. But when we blame God for our suffering that is exactly what we end up doing. Don't give Satan that victory. Instead, put the _______________ on Satan and draw _______________ to God.

9

**TOP REASON #4** We will not be able to trust God.

Developing a trusting relationship with God is vital in all aspects of life, including being able to cope with those dark sky times. But let's face it, that trust relationship will be destroyed if deep down we are blaming God for our suffering.

***Think about a close personal relationship you have. If that person continued to hurt you physically and/or emotionally, could you trust them? Why not?***

The key word here is ____________. In any close relationship, trust is essential. If someone is willfully and continuously hurting us physically and/or emotionally, it is not only impossible, but foolish to trust that person. How could we ever turn to the ______________________ of our hurt for comfort? It simply cannot be done and will only lead to ______________ and______________________. Sadly, countless people have lost trust in God and have bitterly walked away from Him because they have placed the blame for their suffering on the wrong perpetrator.

10

As we move forward in this study, you will see it is ___________ who miraculously fights on our behalf in this broken world. It is God's power that brightens our dark skies. But that will fail miserably and lead to bitterness *if* we are holding onto the false belief that God is the author of our suffering. So, *let that go,* and place the blame for your suffering where it belongs—at the *real* perpetrator—______________. In doing so, you are now ready to move forward in ______________ with your *very real God.* And He *will* brighten those dark skies that Satan has brought into your life.

**IT IS GOD'S POWER THAT BRIGHTENS OUR DARK SKIES.**

**PROCEED WITH READING DR. ANDY'S TREATMENT PLAN ON PAGE 21.**

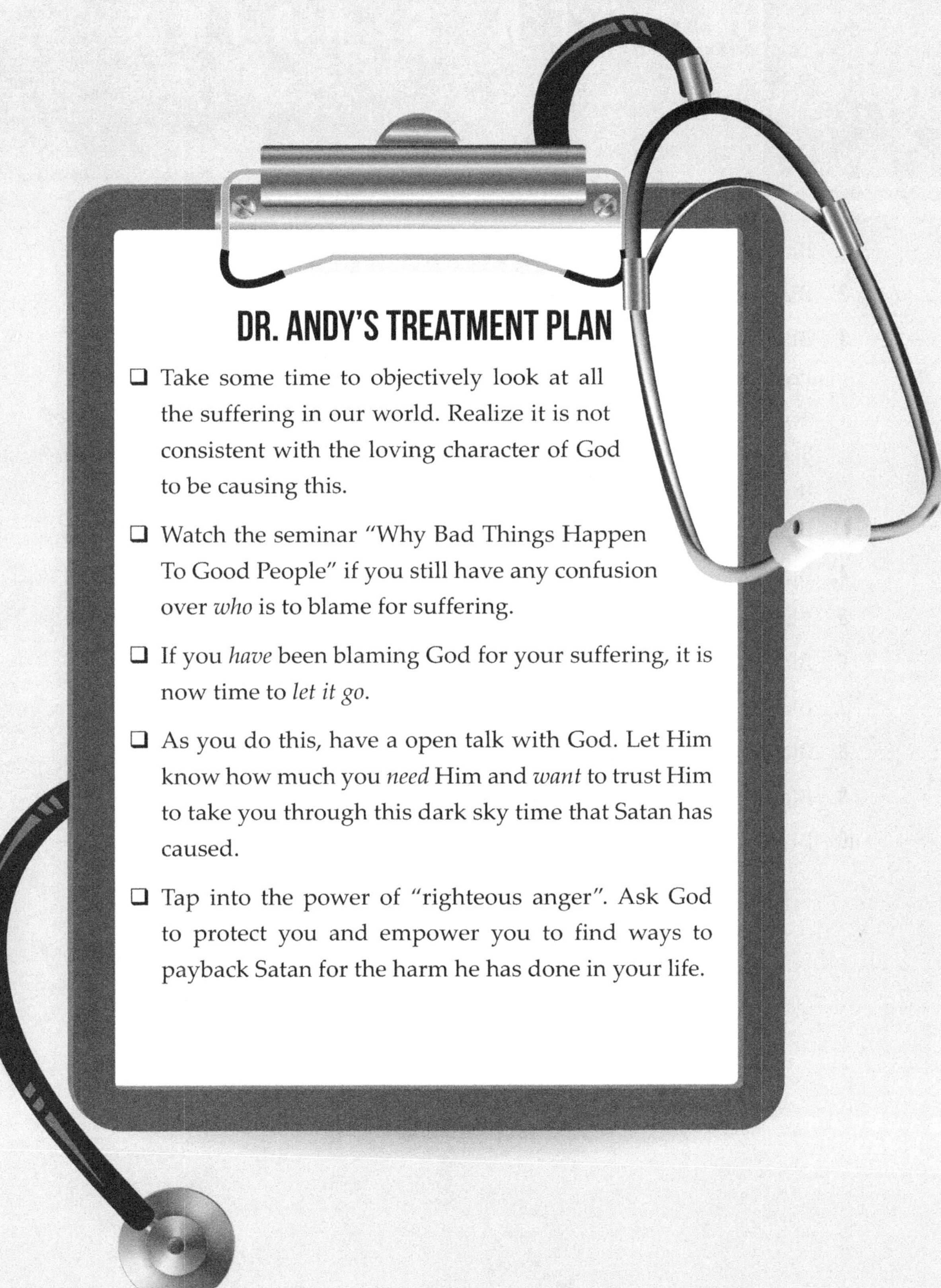

## DR. ANDY'S TREATMENT PLAN

- ❑ Take some time to objectively look at all the suffering in our world. Realize it is not consistent with the loving character of God to be causing this.
- ❑ Watch the seminar "Why Bad Things Happen To Good People" if you still have any confusion over *who* is to blame for suffering.
- ❑ If you *have* been blaming God for your suffering, it is now time to *let it go.*
- ❑ As you do this, have a open talk with God. Let Him know how much you *need* Him and *want* to trust Him to take you through this dark sky time that Satan has caused.
- ❑ Tap into the power of "righteous anger". Ask God to protect you and empower you to find ways to payback Satan for the harm he has done in your life.

# LEADER'S NOTES

1. Blanks: discipline, love
2. Blanks: cause, effect, love, repent, continue
3. Blanks: no fault

   Possible tragedies: 1. Pandemics/plagues 2. cancer 3. heart disease 4. childhood diseases 5. mental illness 6. starvation 7. catastrophic injuries 8. financial demise 9. divorce 10. death of loved ones 11. "Acts of nature" (hurricanes, tornadoes, earthquakes, tsunamis) 12. terrorism/wars etc.

   Blanks: broken, evil
4. Blanks: evil one, Satan, death, lost, expected, Heaven, eventually, Satan
5. Blanks: anger, emotionally, double victory, trust
6. Blanks: powerful, expose, stand, change
7. Blanks: responsible, bitterness
8. Blanks: blame, closer
9. Blanks: trust, perpetrator, anger, bitterness
10. Blanks: God, Satan, trust

STEP 3

# *Prepare For The Dark Skies*

*It is the battles that we do not see coming that are the most devastating.*

# GROUP DISCUSSION

Welcome to Step 3: Prepare For The Dark Skies. Let's begin with prayer (you can use the one below as a guide).

*Father, we understand that in this broken world we will have struggles and at times our skies will turn dark. Help us Father, not to be taken by surprise when this happens. But instead, we ask that You prepare us ahead of time, so that we may prevail over whatever the enemy throws our way. Give us wisdom on how to do that through this lesson. In Jesus Name, Amen.*

(Answers to blanks found on page 32.)

**1**

I was 38 years old, and life was firing on all cylinders. I was working two jobs as a physician and a pastor. My wife, Cyndi, and I were juggling a household with four small children. We had just started a brand-new east side campus of The Bridge Christian Church. I seemed to be in perfect health with boundless energy. Then one morning I woke up ill. My life suddenly was rocked with a life-changing, devastating illness. It seemed to come out of nowhere.

***It's the battles we do not see coming that are the most devastating. Can you think of some examples in life where that is true?***

***Has this happened to you? Write down at least one example below.***

## AUTHOR'S LIST

In this broken world, problems can suddenly come upon us. For example:

1. A serious __________________ can hit us out of the blue.

2. __________________ calamity can strike from nowhere.

3. An unexpected ______________ or serious illness of a loved one.

4. An __________________ may occur causing life-changing limitations.

5. An unexpected ending to a close ____________________________.

These battles and many more are often the most difficult because the surprise factor leaves us totally ____________________________.

**2**

Read 1 Peter 5:8 and John 16:33.

***What is God telling us in these verses about the kind of world we live in? Why do you think He is doing this?***

GOD WANTS HIS KIDS TO BE PREPARED FOR THOSE INEVITABLE BATTLES.

God is telling us that we will have tribulation (or troubles) in this world and that Satan is seeking to strike at any time-to take us by __________________. Why is God telling us this? It is not to scare us into _______________ mode. It is not to create a bunch of Christian __________________. Quite the opposite, God wants us to have a life of ___________ (Psalm 118:24). But He is warning us because He knows those battles that take us by surprise are the most devastating. God wants His kids to be ________________________ and to be spiritually ________________ for those inevitable battles.

3

God gives us helpful direction to prepare for those surprise struggles in life by telling us to, "Consider it pure joy, my brothers and sisters, whenever you face trials of many kinds" (James 1:2 NIV).

***God tells us that we must CONSIDER it pure joy when we face those struggles. Why does He use the word CONSIDER?***

We must *consider* it pure joy because it is ________ joyful. It is painful to go through these difficult struggles. But as you will see, as we proceed with this study, God has this amazing way of bringing ________________ out of the suffering that the enemy throws at us. And when He does this, it is truly wonderful. We therefore can *ultimately* ____________________ it to be pure joy. But, at the time we are going through it—it is anything but joyful.

***What is the significance of God saying when, not if, you face these trials of many kinds?***

Once again, God is alerting us to the reality that these tough times *will* happen. He wants us to be prepared.

4

God said that we will face trials of *"many kinds"*. The best English translation for *many kinds* is "__________________ ___________". God is telling us that our lives will be *polka dotted* with problems of many kinds.

One of the most popular illustrations from *When Skies Aren't Blue* has been the "Canvas of Life".

# THE CANVAS OF LIFE

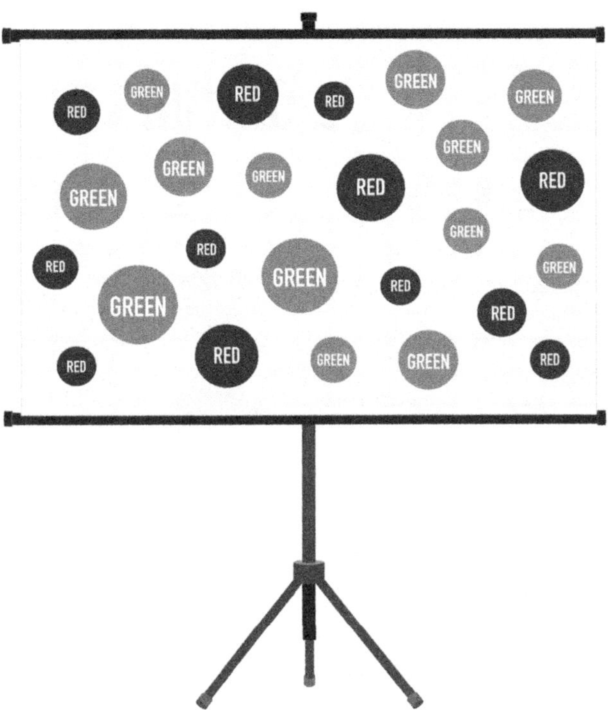


***What do you think it means that our life canvas will have both red (bad things in life) and green (good things in life) dots?***

Life is *not* always wonderful all the time (nothing but green dots). Life is *not* always awful all the time (nothing but red dots). They both exist at the ________ ______________. Sometimes life is generally better, and we have more green dots, and our skies seem bluer. Sometimes life is more difficult, and we have more red dots, and our skies are darker. But we will always have ________ red and green dots. That is how life works, and that is how God wants us to see it.

**5** Take a moment to consider your own life canvas. Write down your name and the good things in your life next to the "green" dots and the bad things next to the "red" dots.

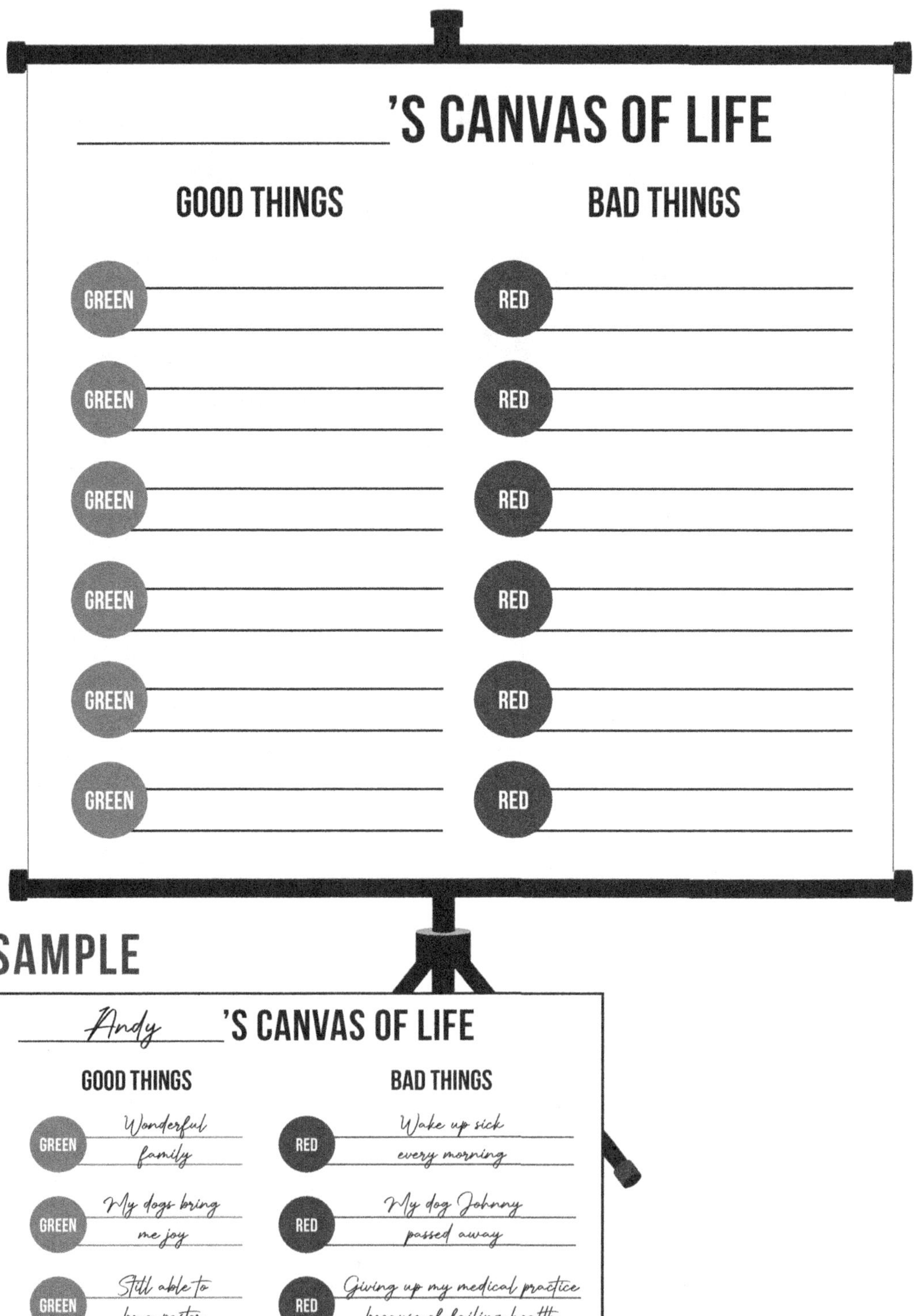

This is how God wants *you* to view your life. Your life has red and green dots (the bad and the good). And those dots are constantly ______________________. The canvas that you just filled in no doubt looks different than it did in your past. And it will be different in the future.

Author's Note

*It will be extremely valuable for you to regularly assess your life by periodically filling in a new life canvas. You can find and print out copies of these canvases at whenskiesarentblue.com.*

***Why do you think God wants you to see your life like the canvas?***

Again, God does not want you to be taken by surprise when the "bad" eventually comes into your life. He wants you to be spiritually and emotionally ______________ for those red dots. Being ready will make all the difference.

6

We will be discussing throughout this study guide many things that we need to have in place to be *ready* for those struggles when they come our way. But for now, let's come up with our *own.*

***List those important things to have in place, so you will be ready when those red dots happen.***

## AUTHOR'S TOP 5 THINGS

1. **GET RIGHT AND LIVE RIGHT FOR GOD.** Getting right with God must be the starting point. We need the power of God and His ________________ ________________ working in our lives to be prepared for those battles when they hit. Please look at whenskiesarentblue.com for more information on that process. After you get right with God, you need to commit to ____________ right for Him.

2. **DEVELOP A GREAT PRAYER LIFE.** Open ________________________________ with God is going to be vital when those struggles hit.

3. **DO NOT BE AN ISLAND CHRISTIAN.** God tells us to ________________________ ourselves with other Christians. There is power in having that strong Christian support structure already in place when those struggles come our way.

4. **BE WELL VERSED IN SCRIPTURE.** Reading and understanding what God has said and promised is going to be vital to handling those red dots. Going through studies such as this will be very helpful for you.

5. **AVOID UNREALISTIC EXPECTATIONS.** A true killer of joy in your life is having unrealistic expectations.

**7** Understand that Satan is going to be throwing red dots at you all the time and wants you to have unrealistic expectations. Let's look at this a little closer by reviewing the diagram below.

VICIOUS CIRCLE

***Why do you think Satan wants you to have unrealistic expectations when it comes to the struggles you face in life?***

Unrealistic expectations of nothing but green dots leads to disenchantment and even bitterness with God when those struggles inevitably hit. And once bitterness sets in, it becomes very easy for Satan to pull you even further away from God (his ______________). We then become easy spiritual prey and our skies grow even darker.

**8** Take a look at this diagram of breaking that vicious circle the enemy uses against us.

VICIOUS CIRCLE BROKEN

***What is the key to breaking that vicious circle, so we do not become easy spiritual prey?***

We ________________ those red dots to be part of our lives. We will not be floored when they inevitably come our way. We will ________________ ahead of time that when the red dots hit, we will cling even tighter to ______________, and become even angrier at ________________. By doing this, we have disarmed one of Satan's greatest weapons against us, pulling us away from God. This type of power happens by expecting and preparing for those red dots.

**PROCEED WITH READING DR. ANDY'S TREATMENT PLAN ON PAGE 33.**

# LEADER'S NOTES

1. Leaders: Encourage them to share their answers with the group.
   Blanks: illness, Financial, death, accident, relationship, unprepared
2. Blanks: surprise, panic, pessimists, joy, prepared, strong
3. Blanks: not, victory, consider
4. Blanks: polka dots, same time, both
5. Blanks: changing, ready
6. Blanks: Holy Spirit, live, communication, surround
7. Blank: goal
8. Blanks: expect, decide, God, Satan

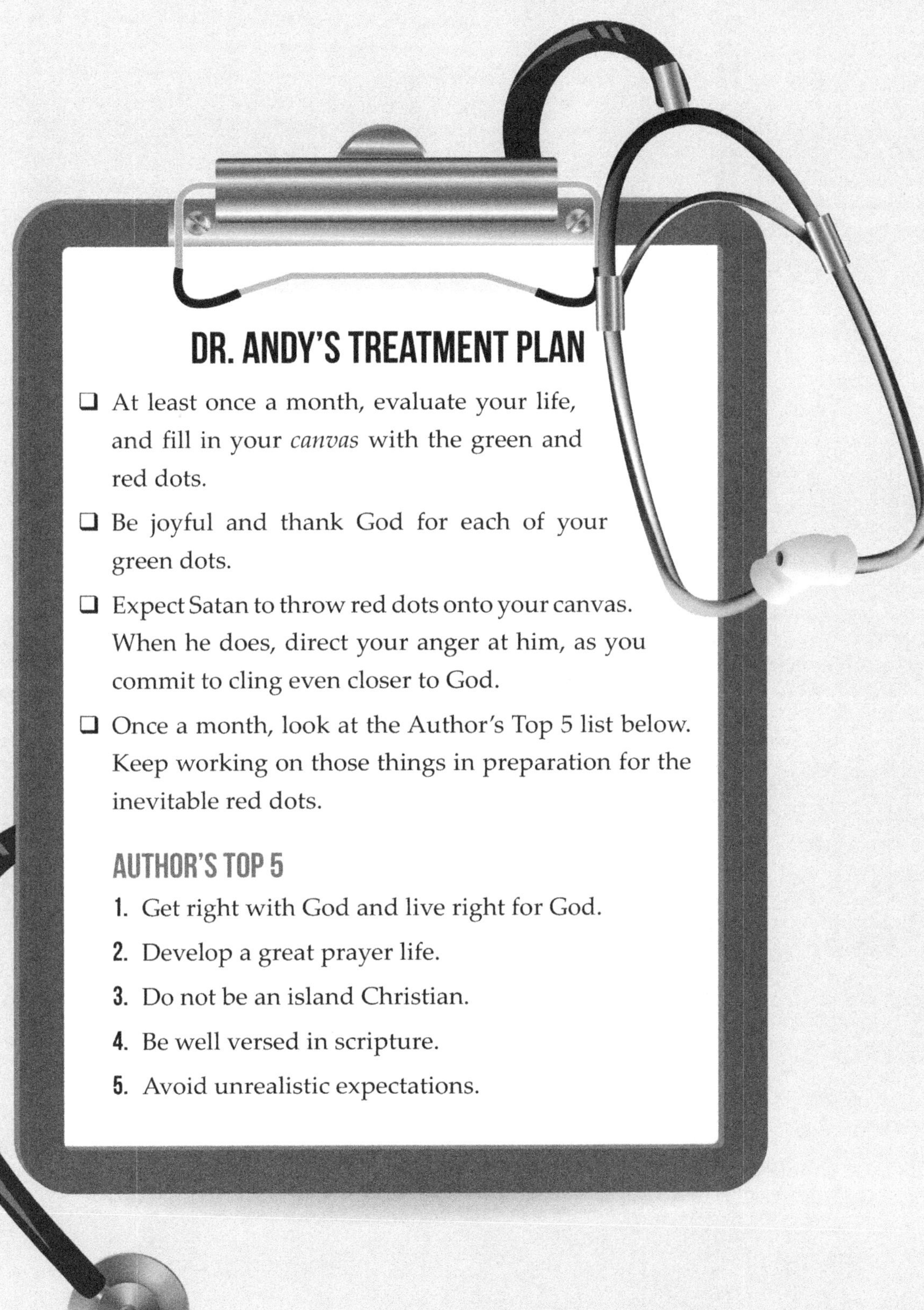

## DR. ANDY'S TREATMENT PLAN

- ❑ At least once a month, evaluate your life, and fill in your *canvas* with the green and red dots.
- ❑ Be joyful and thank God for each of your green dots.
- ❑ Expect Satan to throw red dots onto your canvas. When he does, direct your anger at him, as you commit to cling even closer to God.
- ❑ Once a month, look at the Author's Top 5 list below. Keep working on those things in preparation for the inevitable red dots.

### AUTHOR'S TOP 5

1. Get right with God and live right for God.
2. Develop a great prayer life.
3. Do not be an island Christian.
4. Be well versed in scripture.
5. Avoid unrealistic expectations.

STEP 4

# *Take Action*

*God often brings healing through the actions that we take.*

# GROUP DISCUSSION

**START HERE** Welcome to Step 4: Take Action. Let's begin with prayer (you can use the one below as a guide).

*Father, we know that in this broken world we will face difficulties. But You tell us if we think and plan well, You will direct our steps. So Father, we ask You to give us wisdom through this study to help us take action against our struggles. And You will use that action to help us and brighten our dark skies. In Jesus Name, Amen.*

(Answers to blanks found on page 42.)

**1** "Doctors make the worst patients." Guilty as charged. That was true for me. I rarely, if ever, went to the doctor. And that worked just fine, until *I got sick.* I recognized very quickly that the complexity of my illness was far beyond what I could handle alone. I needed help. I needed others. I needed to take action.

If you are familiar with my story in *When Skies Aren't Blue,* you know that the medical care I received saved my life. Was it a complete cure? No. This is a chronic disease for which there is no cure (bonus if you remember the disease). But the treatment got me to the point where I could at least eat enough to survive. The medication allowed me to be able to stand up again, without losing consciousness. This wonderful care brought me at least some semblance of life. I am very grateful for that.

***If I decided that I was just going to sit back and take no action, what do you think the outcome would have been?***

I would not have survived. My wife would not have had a husband. My four small kids would not have had a dad. My church would not have had me as their pastor. And I would not have written this book to help others who are suffering. I can't stress this enough, when we face those big red dots in our lives, we cannot sit passively back and do nothing. We need to be proactive and "__________ __________________".

**2** God certainly has weighed in on the importance of our taking action. He says in Proverbs 16:9, "The mind of man [a person] plans his way, but the Lord directs his steps."

***So, what is God saying here about our responsibility when it comes to dealing with the issues that life throws our way?***

God expects us to ______________ well, _____________ and take action (*the mind of a person plans his way*). But then God steps in and ____________________ that action/plan (*the Lord directs his steps*).

He does not want us to sit back and _____________ ________________________ when it comes to those red dot struggles in our lives. He expects us to act and apply His principles to whatever we are going through.

**GOD EXPECTS US TO THINK WELL, PLAN AND TAKE ACTION.**

**3** Some may say that by taking action on our own, we are bypassing God.

***Do you think that is true? Are we leaving God out of the equation if we are initiating action?***

We are not bypassing God. It is still the ________________ of ____________ that is at work. He often uses the actions we take to bring healing and resolution to our struggles. We are eliminating a powerful tool that God uses if we choose to passively sit back and do nothing about those red dots in our lives.

**4** Now let's talk about how you can apply this principle to the struggles in your life.

***What are the red dots in your life? Write them down and then write down some potential actions that you could take to deal with those struggles.***

| STRUGGLES | ACTIONS I CAN TAKE |
|---|---|
| RED ________________________ | ________________________ |
| RED ________________________ | ________________________ |
| RED ________________________ | ________________________ |

Here are some common examples that I came up with:

| STRUGGLES | ACTIONS I CAN TAKE |
|---|---|
| RED Physical/Medical Illness | See a ____________________. |
| RED Psychiatric/Emotional Illness | Seek out ________________ care. |

*Note: So often people assume that psychiatric issues are spiritual problems. While depression, anxiety and other psychiatric struggles may have a spiritual component to them, the problem is often an imbalance of chemicals in the brain (neurotransmitters). Medical care is vital for this.*

| | | |
|---|---|---|
| RED | Marital/Family/ Relational Issues | Seek out ________ ________________ from an appropriate therapist/counselor, pastor or trusted friend. |
| RED | Financial Issues | Seek out counsel from those with ________________________ expertise, who could give sound, Biblically based financial direction. |
| RED | Grief | Grief tends to push us towards ___________________________. Avoid that. Isolation will make the grieving worse. To help walk you through this difficult process, seek out a trusted friend, wise counselor, pastor, etc. |
| RED | Loneliness | There is a vicious cycle when it comes to loneliness. We have a desire not to be alone. Yet the very act of being alone makes it even harder to connect with others. And a virtual (social media) connection is not the same as the real thing. It still leaves many people feeling alone. One of the most effective ways to break the loneliness cycle is going to a physical ______________ (not online) and getting connected with other Christians. |

**5** For many of the struggles we face in life, "action" is often that of seeking out appropriate help or counsel. This is part of God's plan for us (read Proverbs 15:22).

***What is God telling us about the potential outcome of our struggles if we decide to not get appropriate help/counsel?***

God said that success or failure is often dependent upon wise counsel. He can bring success through those actions. There are many scriptures where God stresses the importance of seeking out wise counsel for our struggles. Here are a few: Proverbs 11:14, 12:15 and 19:20-21.

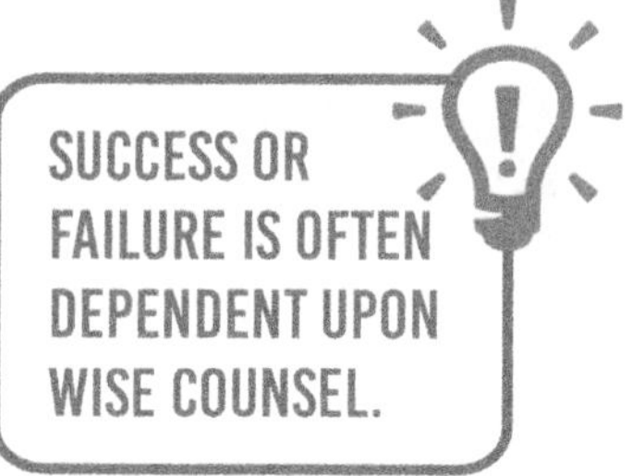


**6** God often brings wonderful and even miraculous healing to those red dot struggles in our lives through wise actions that we take. Of course, we should be grateful to Him when that happens. But there are times when we take action, but the problem remains.

***Why is that? Come up with at least one reason why the struggles may remain, despite the actions we have taken.***

## AUTHOR'S TOP 5 REASONS

Here are some reasons that I have observed in my years of ministry and medicine.

1. Those struggling have ________ gotten right with God.

   God certainly blesses His kids. But we are not automatically God's kid (read Romans 5:10). This tells us that until we are ______________________________ to God, we are God's ____________. We become God's kids when we get right with Him (reconciled) through what Jesus did for us on the cross. We cannot expect those blessings from God until we first get right with Him.

   (See whenskiesarentblue.com for the process of getting right with God.)

2. The struggle is a result of ongoing ________.

   We discussed this back in Step 2. Sometimes the struggles in our lives are a result of discipline from our Heavenly Dad who is trying to get us back on the right path again. If that is the case, the solution is ________________________.

**3.** The actions taken may not be wise or may even be ____________________.

We cannot expect God to bless actions that are ____________________ to His principles. The more aligned our actions are with His principles—the greater the chance for success. If we are receiving counsel, make sure it is grounded in Biblical wisdom.

**4.** Resolution of these struggles may take ________.

We want our struggles resolved instantaneously. But remember, God does not work on our time schedule. In addition, there is so much happening behind the scenes that we cannot begin to fathom (read Daniel 10:12-13). Because of a supernatural battle, an angel was __________________ from being able to help Daniel. I believe God shared this story with us in scripture to show us that in this temporary world, evil has very real power, which at times will delay God's help.

We need to learn the power of __________________ waiting on God, knowing He is fighting for His kids on that supernatural level.

**LEARN THE POWER OF PATIENTLY WAITING ON GOD.**

**5.** Not every problem will be completely ____________ in this broken world.

We are not in Heaven yet. Despite all our "actions", there will be times that the struggles remain (either completely or partially).

This was certainly the case with me. God used the medical action that I took to bring some healing. I am very grateful for that. But the disease is still present. The suffering continues. To find those blue skies, despite the ongoing struggles, I need to continue to apply all that we will be discussing in the remainder of this study guide.

We have so much more to learn together!

**PROCEED WITH READING DR. ANDY'S TREATMENT PLAN ON PAGE 43.**

# LEADER'S NOTES

1. Name of Andy's disease: dysautonomia (dis-ot-ə-nō-mē-ə): Dysautonomia is an umbrella term used to describe several different medical conditions that cause a malfunction of the Autonomic Nervous System. Andy suffers from a form of dysautonomia called Postural Orthostatic Tachycardic Syndrome (POTS).
   Blanks: take action
2. Blanks: think, plan, directs, do nothing
3. Blanks: power, God
4. Leaders: Please give the group plenty of time to answer this question. Have them specifically write down their current red dot issues and then some potential actions they could take to effectively deal with those struggles. They may or may not want to share their answers but do encourage them to share if they feel comfortable.
   Blanks: physician, medical, wise counsel, financial, isolation, church
6. Blanks: not, reconciled, enemies, sin, repentance, unbiblical, opposed, time, delayed, patiently, fixed

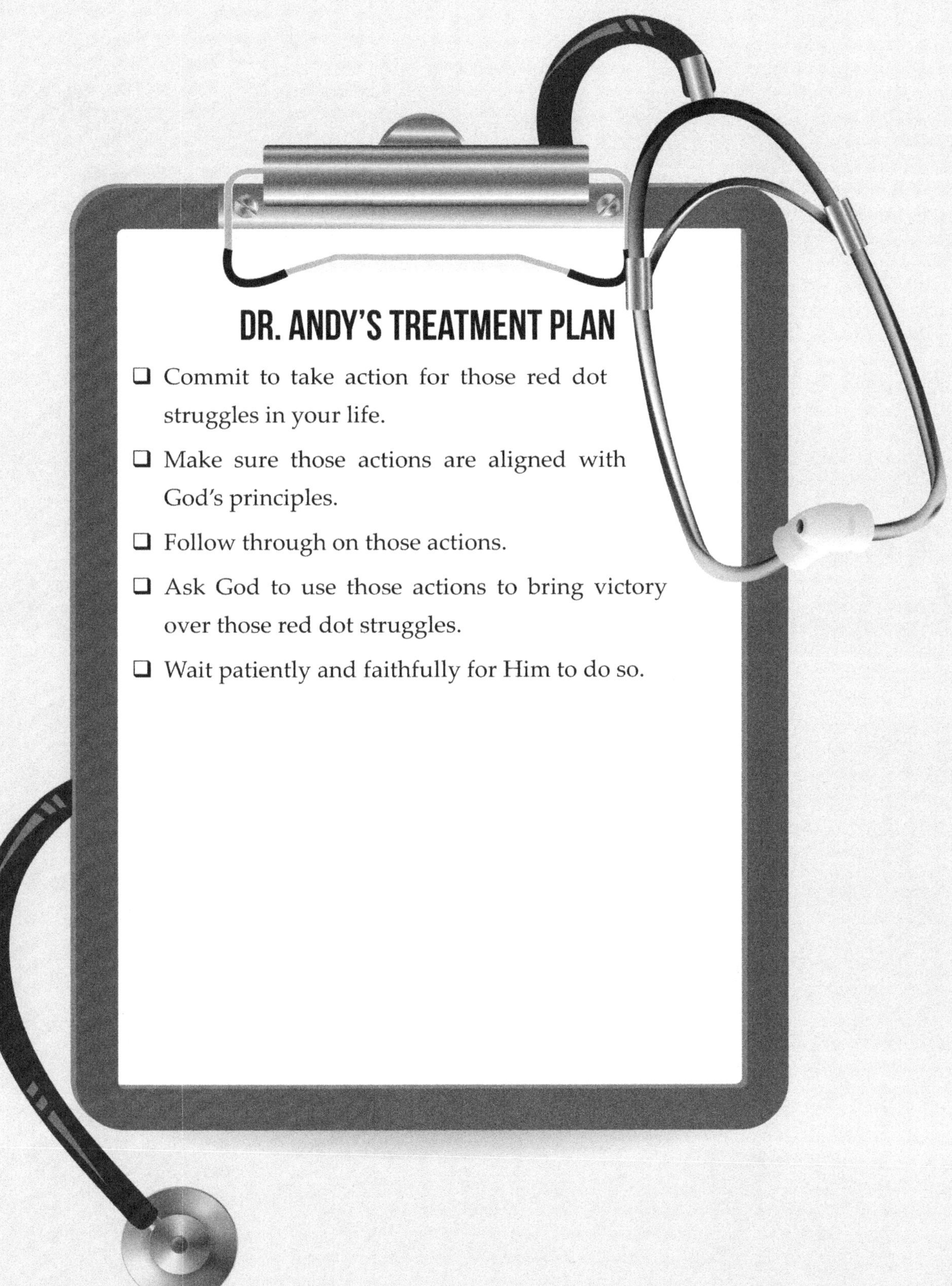

## DR. ANDY'S TREATMENT PLAN

- ❑ Commit to take action for those red dot struggles in your life.
- ❑ Make sure those actions are aligned with God's principles.
- ❑ Follow through on those actions.
- ❑ Ask God to use those actions to bring victory over those red dot struggles.
- ❑ Wait patiently and faithfully for Him to do so.

STEP 5

# *Let The Old Life Go*

*Our skies will never turn blue if the specter of our old lives keeps us from living our new lives.*

# GROUP DISCUSSION

**START HERE** Congratulations, you have now reached Step 5 in finding those *blue skies.* That is the good news. Now for the tough news. This is arguably the most difficult of all the Steps—at least it was for me—letting go of the old life! Let's begin with prayer (you can use the one below as a guide).

> *Father, things can so easily move to another level of darkness when we realize that our struggles may be unchangeable. We long so much for our old lost lives, and we can find ourselves in a very dark place. I ask that through this lesson, You give us wisdom and direction to help us truly let go of our old lives and embrace our new lives with You. We ask that You teach us to find joy, regardless of what our ongoing struggles may be. In Jesus Name, Amen.*

(Answers to blanks found on page 54.)

**1** As we learned in the last Step, we need to take action to deal with our red dot struggles. I certainly did. There was some improvement but it was not a cure. The miserable nausea continued. I would have ongoing cardiac arrhythmias (irregular heartbeats). Brain fog, dizziness and fatigue would still be overwhelming. I still would not be able to stay upright for any prolonged period. The energy and abilities of the previously healthy young man were gone. This was now going to be my life.

***What would your initial reaction be if you were in my place?***

2 I found myself slipping into a very dark place. It was not so much the physical suffering that sent me there, instead, it was the realization that the things I used to be able to do and accomplish would be no longer. I would lay in my room for weeks at a time, lights out, staring into the darkness and nothingness of the ceiling. That is how I felt, just dark, with no hope.

***Have you experienced this in your own life? What was that like for you?***

3 We know in this broken world that the enemy will constantly challenge us with those red dot struggles. And sadly, we also know that some of those struggles may become unchangeable (at least in this life).

***What are some of those the struggles that can become unchangeable?***

## AUTHOR'S LIST

Here is my list of some of those unchangeable struggles that can so easily send us to that very dark emotional place.

1. Chronic ________________ issues with significant limitations (physical or mental health issues).
2. ________________ over the loss of someone very close.
3. ____________________ calamity.
4. ________________ can easily destroy our hopes and dreams in life.
5. _________________________ from a family member or close friend.

There are many "unchangeable struggles" in this broken world which can radically and permanently (at least in this life) alter our lives for the worse.

**4** The depth of despair from these unchangeable struggles can be overwhelming.

***How can you cope with this level of darkness?***
***How can you find __________ again?***
***How can you ______________ ____________***
***from those chains of darkness?***

> DESPAIR FROM THESE UNCHANGEABLE STRUGGLES CAN BE OVERWHELMING.

Well, if you read *When Skies Aren't Blue*, you know that I quoted of all people, Dumbledore (from Harry Potter) who said, "Happiness can be found, even in the darkest times, if one only remembers to turn on the light."

**5** There you go. Just turn on the light; easier said than done, Dumbledore. But how do we go about doing it?

***Can you come up with a list of things to help "turn on the light" when we find ourselves in that dark place, lamenting over the life that is no longer?***

Trying to find that light switch can be very challenging. I have been there. It is difficult, but certainly possible. Let me give you my ***7 key steps*** to turning on that light and letting go of the past.

## AUTHOR'S 7 KEY STEPS

1. You will need the ________________ of God.
2. Do not attempt to do it ________________.
3. Give yourself time to ________________.
4. Do not accept a life without ______________.
5. Do not let ________________ win.
6. Take your ________________ captive to obey God.
7. ________________ this is now your life.

Now, let's look at each of these steps in more detail.

6

**STEP 1:** You will need the power of God. Human will power alone cannot conquer this depth of darkness (read Acts 2:38).

HUMAN WILL POWER CANNOT CONQUER THIS DARKNESS.

***What is the gift that God says we receive when we go through that process of getting right with Him?***

When we get right with God and make Christ the Lord and Savior of our lives, we receive His Holy Spirit. That is the ______________ we will need. Without the power of God's Spirit in our lives, we will be stuck in the darkness. If you are not sure if you have gone through the process of getting right with God, please go to whenskiesarentblue.com for more information.

7

**STEP 2:** Do not attempt to do it alone. When we find ourselves in that level of darkness, we do not ______________ well. We need help from others. I was so despondent over the loss of my healthy life, that I couldn't find my way out of the darkness on my own. I am so thankful that I had my friend and our founding pastor, David McAllister, to guide me. I encourage you to read/reread that story with Pastor McAllister in *When Skies Aren't Blue* (pages 58-61). It was a very personal, painful and emotional time. But I shared that story because I knew it could be helpful for those who are stuck in that darkness.

***Where can we find people who can help guide us to find that switch?***

Author's Note

*I would not necessarily suggest that you have a family member try and walk you through this. Sometimes, they are just too close to the situation to be objective and do and say what is needed.*

God gave us the ______________ to be a tremendous source of power and encouragement for us. If you find yourself in the darkness of an unchangeable struggle, then it is vital that you get plugged into a Bible-based, Christian church. Seek the help and the counsel the church will provide for you.

8

**STEP 3:** Give yourself time to grieve. I did. In fact—I wailed. I wailed for the life that was no longer. I wailed for all that this disease has taken from me. I wailed for the days of health that were gone. I wailed for it all.

But then it was time to ________ ______ ______. Give yourself time to grieve over whatever this unchangeable struggle has taken from you. But there comes a time when we must just *let it go.*

***Why can it be difficult to just "let it go"?***

9

**STEP 4:** Do not accept a life without joy. Some may think that it is a contradiction to both have joy and an unchangeable struggle going on at the same time. Usually, confusion occurs because we equate joy with happiness.

***What do you think the difference is between joy and happiness?***

Happiness is an ______________________ or a feeling. It depends on the circumstances around us. If things are going well and we have nothing but green dots in our lives, then yes, we can *feel happy.*

Joy on the other hand is a state of ______________________. This happens at the deepest level of our souls. It is not a feeling or emotion, like happiness. It is far more powerful and ______________________ in nature.

God has promised us that if we trust and depend on Him, we can have ________. He has not promised happiness. In fact, He has told us that in this broken world, we will have red dot struggles, sometimes unchangeable ones. And let's be honest, when we do, they will make us feel anything but happy. It is only from the power of God that we can have that incredible *joy*, regardless of the struggle.

> ***Read Psalm 118:24. What does this say about God's expectations for us when it comes to being joyful.***

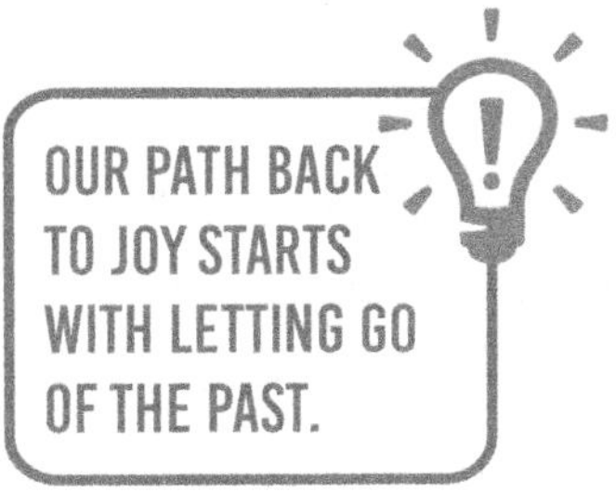


God ______________ us to *rejoice* in the day He has given us. We will be discussing many principles in the remainder of this study guide that will help us to have that joy from God, even during dark times. But we will *not* be able to find that joy if we allow the specter of our old healthy life to keep on haunting us. Our path back to joy starts with letting go of the past.

**10**

**STEP 5:** Do not let Satan win. It is Satan who struck me with this horrible disease. It is Satan who took so much of my life away. It is Satan who put my family through this ordeal of having to watch their husband/father suffer so much. And if I ever wanted to pay Satan back for what he had done, then I had to let go of the past, and start ________________ for ______________.

It is the same for you. If you want to pay Satan back for that awful struggle in your life, then you need to decide to let go of the *old life* and embrace the new one (limitations and all).

**11** **STEP 6:** Take your thoughts captive to obey God. We must ____________ and constantly challenge ourselves to think the way God wants us to. God does not want us to mentally live in the old life. God wants us to find joy in our new lives, regardless of the struggles and limitations.

> ***Read 2 Corinthians 10:5. How can you apply this to the concept of letting the old life go?***

Recognize that this is ultimately a spiritual battle for your ____________. Every time those thoughts of longing for the old life creep back into your head, __________ _________ ___________ immediately. Those are harmful thoughts and are from the enemy. Take those destructive thoughts captive to God and ask Him to help you to think clearly.

**12** **STEP 7:** Accept this is now your life. We must deep down, and honestly ___________ our new lives. To keep me grounded, every morning I challenge myself with certain questions: "Will I be sick today?" Yes, but this is my life. "Will I be limited today?" Yes, but this is my life. "Can I have joy even with these limitations?" Yes. "Can I still make a difference in my life, even being sick?" Yes.

I decided to no longer let what I *can't* do interfere with what I *can* do. And yes, deep down I have learned to fully accept and embrace this new sick and limited life.

DO NOT LET WHAT YOU CAN'T DO INTERFERE WITH WHAT YOU CAN DO.

> ***Whatever the unchangeable struggles are in your life, are you ready to let them go?***

Once you have truly accepted those unchangeables, then you indeed have flipped _____ that switch. You are now ready to let go of the past and start moving forward with the power of God in your new life.

**PROCEED WITH READING DR. ANDY'S TREATMENT PLAN ON PAGE 53.**

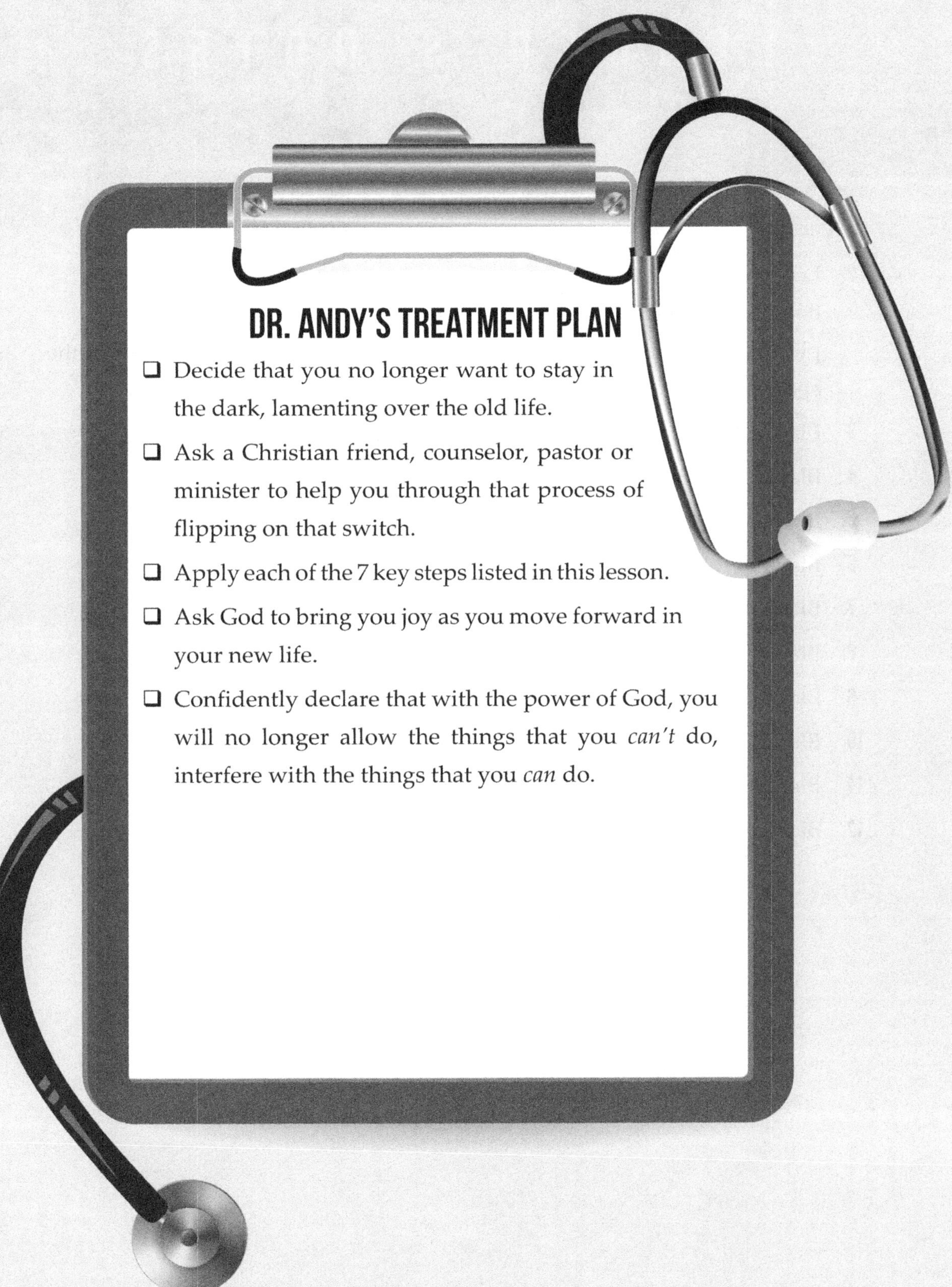

## DR. ANDY'S TREATMENT PLAN

- ❑ Decide that you no longer want to stay in the dark, lamenting over the old life.
- ❑ Ask a Christian friend, counselor, pastor or minister to help you through that process of flipping on that switch.
- ❑ Apply each of the 7 key steps listed in this lesson.
- ❑ Ask God to bring you joy as you move forward in your new life.
- ❑ Confidently declare that with the power of God, you will no longer allow the things that you *can't* do, interfere with the things that you *can* do.

# LEADER'S NOTES

2. Leaders: Some in the group may not feel comfortable sharing. This very dark time can be quite personal. But even if they do not want to share, please encourage them to write those experiences and feelings down in the space provided.
3. Blanks: health, Grief, Financial, Divorce, Estrangement
4. Blanks: joy, break free
5. Blanks: power, alone, grieve, joy, Satan, thoughts, Accept
6. Blank: power
7. Blanks: think, church
8. Blanks: let it go
9. Blanks: emotion, well-being, spiritual, joy, expects
10. Blanks: living, today,
11. Blanks: actively, mind, shut them down
12. Blanks: accept, on

STEP 6

# *Redefine Victory Over Today*

*How can we find victory when we feel so lousy?*
*We redefine victory!*

# GROUP DISCUSSION

Welcome to Step 6. We are ready to take a very key step forward in finding those blue skies in the midst of our ongoing struggles. Let's start with prayer (you can use the one below as a guide).

*Father, so many struggles can keep us from accomplishing the things that we used to be able to do. This can be so discouraging. Please give us wisdom in this lesson to learn to redefine victory. And as we do, help us to transform that discouragement into joy and contentment. In Jesus Name, Amen.*

(Answers to blanks found on page 64.)

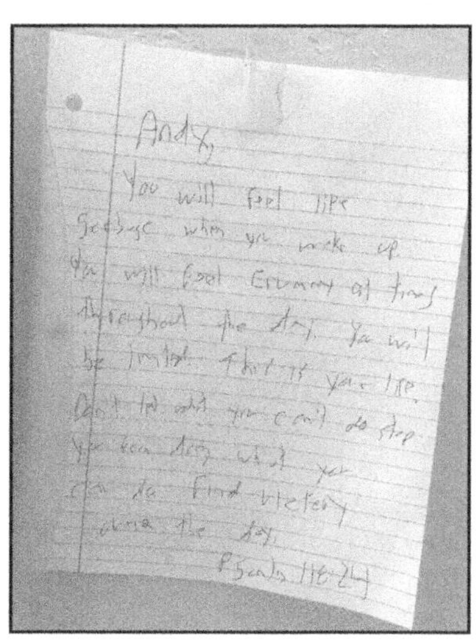


**1**

I have taped this letter on my bathroom mirror. It is the first thing that I see in the morning when I wake up. In case you can't read my doctor writing, it says: "Andy, you will feel like garbage when you wake up. You will feel crummy at times throughout the day. This is your life. Don't let what you can't do, stop you from doing what you can do. Find victory over the day. Psalm 118:24".

***Why do you think I place this in a location where it is the first thing I see in the morning?***

Hopefully you didn't say, "So Andy doesn't see his awful bed head first thing in the morning." But the real reason I place the note in that location is based on what we discussed in Step 5—letting the old life go.

Every morning I wake up, and I remind myself that the old, healthy life is gone, and sickness and limitations are now expected in this new life. But I am not going to let what I ________ do stop me from doing what I ________ do. I am not going to let those limitations and struggles stop me from having the ________ and victory that God wants me to have (read Psalm 118:24).

2 Okay, so I am reminding myself that I am sick, and I will feel crummy in this new life. But here is a fair question:

***How can we possibly have victory when we know our struggle is going to limit us?***

We are going to need to ________________ victory. Let's dig into this important principle.

3 Prior to getting sick, I was working two full time jobs as an ER radiologist and a pastor. Cyndi and I were raising four small children. I was still playing competitive racquetball. I seemed to have endless energy.

Then this illness hit and everything changed. Suddenly, just finding the strength to stand up was a challenge. How could I possibly find victory with this level of limitation, given what I was used to doing? The answer, as mentioned above, is I had to redefine victory.

*What did that look like?* Sometimes, it was just waking up and getting out of bed—a victory! Maybe running a simple errand—a victory! I couldn't keep up with my kids athletically any longer, but just going to their games—a victory! I could no longer run an entire church as a pastor. But I could gather my strength to attend church, and minister to others the best I could—a victory! I had to dial things way back and *redefine* what a *victory* was for me.

***What about you? What are things that you can realistically accomplish (limitations and all) and call it a victory?***

Remember, your victory doesn't have to be some ________________ accomplishment. It can be a ____________________ chore or something ___________ like a hobby. Sometimes just making sure we get our ________________ and Bible reading time in is a victory. Perhaps it is reaching out to spend some _________ with your spouse, child, family member or friend. If you are still employed, then maybe it is just getting through the workday, even if it was a struggle. You did it! Whatever it is . . . find the thing that you can *do*, and then do it.

Satan is going to try and convince you that in order for you to have victory, it has to be a major accomplishment, like you used to be able to do. Don't let him pull you back into the darkness and lament the old healthy life. Remember, you let that life go. Redefine your victories based on what you ____________ do.

**4** God created us to be ________________. When we are not fulfilling that, we end up suffering physically, emotionally, spiritually or psychologically.

***According to this diagram, what happens if we end up doing nothing but lament over what we can no longer do?***

FAILING HEALTH
LAMENTING WHAT WE CAN'T DO
REDEFINE VICTORY
DEPRESSION AND ANXIETY
PERSONAL SATISFACTION
EXACERBATES THE ILLNESS
GREATER INNER PEACE WITH ILLNESS
DARKER SKIES
REDEFINE VICTORY
BLUER SKIES

If we do nothing but lament over what we have lost, it just leads to even _______________ __________. This is exactly what Satan desires for your life.

***If we redefine victory, what is the ultimate outcome?***

One of the keys to finding _____________ __________, when the enemy has thrown some awful red dots into your life, is redefining victory. And then having the courage to _________ on it. You will be astonished at the personal satisfaction and inner _____________ that this will bring you.

One of the barriers that keeps us from being able to successfully redefine victory is not _______________ ______ of the old healthy life. If you are still struggling with this, please put into place those principles in Step 5. I can't stress this enough; you will not be able to move forward and find victory until you truly let go of the *old life*.

5 Holding onto the old life is a mental scheme that the enemy uses against us. But another one of his mind games is to get us to worry about *tomorrow* (read Matthew 6:34).

***What does Jesus say about worrying about tomorrow?***

The God who created us and knows us inside and out said don't _______________ about tomorrow. We need to deal with today. Jesus is challenging us to just concentrate on whatever your victory is for today, and don't even consider tomorrow.

***When we deal with struggles and limitations, why do you think worrying about tomorrow is so harmful?***

When I start worrying about all the things that tomorrow can potentially bring, and how I can possibly handle those things, I become _________________________ and emotionally deflated. And then my motivation for even finding victory *today* is gone. This is what the enemy wants. So, don't go there. Do not even think about tomorrow. Just focus on the victories you can tackle for today—just today.

**6** Please remember that this is a battle for the mind, and we must take our thoughts captive to obey God and listen to His voice (2 Corinthians 10:5). Satan wants your mind to be consumed with the fact that you used to be able to accomplish so much more. He wants you to worry about the *tomorrows* of life. Shut those thoughts down completely. Do not let them in. You have a choice!

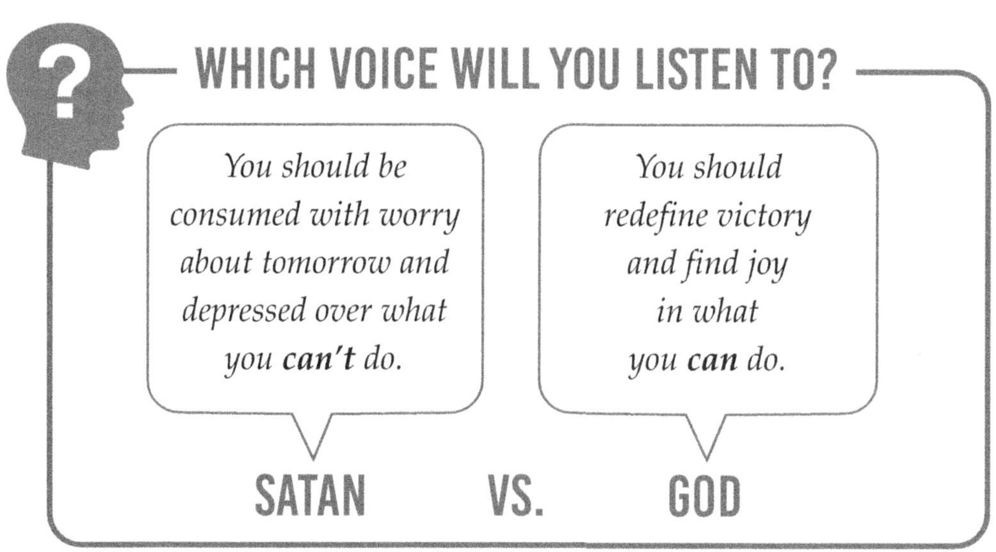

**7** One of the things that I commonly hear from people who chronically struggle is that *doing* these things is *so hard.* Never forget: the fact that it was a struggle makes you so much more ____________ for doing it.

***Why is it heroic?***

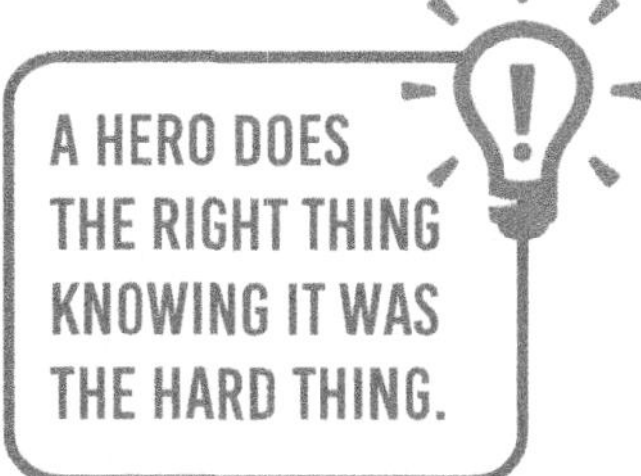


I think one of the best definitions of a *hero* is someone who does the ____________ thing, knowing it is the ___________ thing. Knowing it was going to be a struggle, you still redefined victory and did it. That is *heroic*. Do not let Satan negate that. He will try to convince you that your achievement should have been easy. Perhaps in your old life. But this is your new life. And the very fact you did the right thing, even though it was the hard thing—that is heroic in the eyes of God. Way to go!

I have counseled people who are struggling with limitations, and they get upset that a simple chore like getting their kids to school in the morning was so overwhelming and exhausting. I ask them, "Well, did you do it and get them to school?" And when they tell me that they did, I tell them how heroic that was. We must see ourselves as those heroes who do the right thing even though it was difficult. It makes a huge difference in __________________________ our skies.

8 In addition to being heroic, redefining victory can also bring a sense of fulfillment in life.

***Can you think of why redefining victory and focusing on those "easier" things might lead to that sense of fulfillment?***

When I was healthy and *burning the candle at both ends,* I went to bed at night, exhausted, and thinking of all the things that I *still* needed to do. But now, while I am still exhausted, I fall asleep proud of what I did accomplish. We start to learn to appreciate and take joy in the things that we ________ accomplish and not worry about all the things left undone. It is a fulfilling way to approach life.

9 As we choose to redefine those victories and then heroically do them, something astounding begins to happen. And that is, despite our limitations and our struggles, we will start to have a real sense of ________________________ in life. And one amazing day, you are going to look up and notice that your skies aren't so dark anymore.

PROCEED WITH READING DR. ANDY'S TREATMENT PLAN ON PAGE 63.

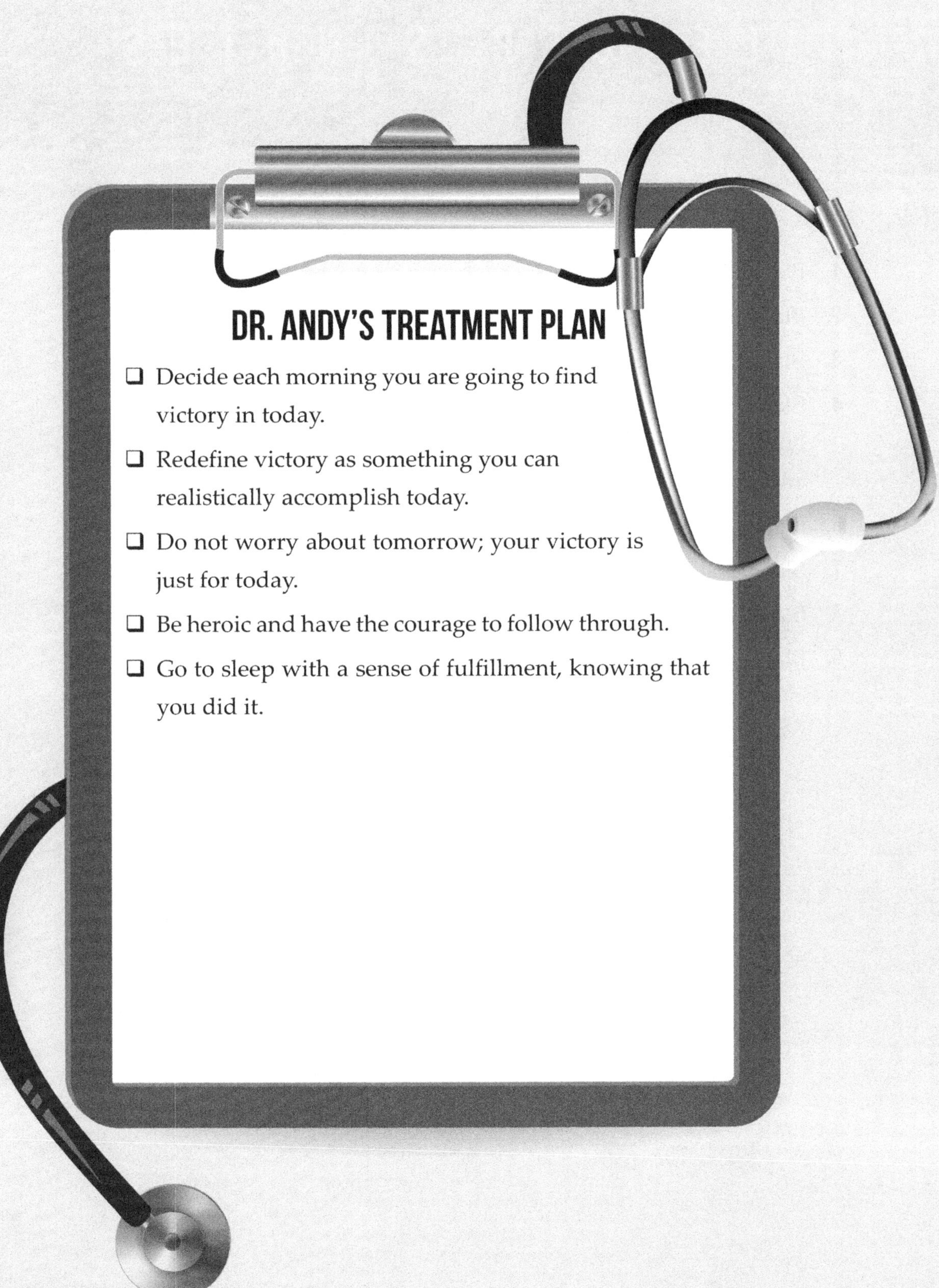

## DR. ANDY'S TREATMENT PLAN

- ❑ Decide each morning you are going to find victory in today.
- ❑ Redefine victory as something you can realistically accomplish today.
- ❑ Do not worry about tomorrow; your victory is just for today.
- ❑ Be heroic and have the courage to follow through.
- ❑ Go to sleep with a sense of fulfillment, knowing that you did it.

# LEADER'S NOTES

1. Blanks: can't, can, joy
2. Blank: redefine
3. Blanks: major, simple, fun, prayer, time, can
4. Blanks: doing, darker skies, blue skies, act, peace, letting go
   Leaders: Have the group refer to the "Redefine Victory" diagram to answer the questions.
5. Blanks: worry, overwhelmed
7. Blanks: heroic, right, hard, brightening
8. Blank: did
9. Blank: contentment

STEP 7

# *Watch God Light It Up In Unexpected Ways*

*God is the God of "it just so happened".*

# GROUP DISCUSSION

**START HERE** Welcome to Step 7 in our journey to finding those blue skies. This Step is one of the most rewarding, as we will learn to watch God work through our struggles and brighten our skies. But we can easily be blinded from seeing God in action. Let's study this lesson together to make sure this does not happen to us. Begin with prayer (you can use the one below as a guide).

*Father, sometimes we can get so immersed in our struggles that we are unable to see You at work. I pray that through this lesson, You will help us to know that Your heart breaks for our suffering. We are not alone, and You are walking us through those tough times. You are the God of all those just so happened moments. Help us see that clearly. In Jesus Name, Amen.*

(Answers to blanks found on page 74.)

**1** People sometimes gravitate towards the ______________________, when it comes to their struggles and God.

**EXTREME 1:** "God needs to heal all my struggles, completely and instantly."

**EXTREME 2:** "God is powerless to heal my struggles in this broken world."

There are spiritual dangers in either of those extremes.

***What is the danger of believing Extreme 1 as truth?***

**2** This extreme will eventually lead to spiritual ________________________. If God completely and instantly healed all our struggles, then we would be back in paradise. This would be heaven on earth. And we know for now, that is not the case. Quite the opposite: God has told us we will have problems and struggles. It is not an accurate expectation that God will fix all our struggles, completely and instantly. This type of false expectation will cause our skies to grow __________________.

***What is the danger of believing Extreme 2 as truth?***

This is also not a biblically accurate view. Scripture clearly shows God supporting His kids in this broken world. If we truly believe that God is powerless to heal our struggles, we end up __________________ __________ on some amazing blessings of God.

**3** I want to take you through an exercise that I think demonstrates how God is actively working through our struggles in this broken world.

***Think about your past struggles. List some of those struggles here.***

***How are those struggles going today?***

We all have had many problems over the years. And at the time, they were so concerning and even overwhelming for us. Yet, for many of those things, they are a distant memory. God handled them. There is spiritual power in ______________________ and ______________________ God for all those times He *has* come through and dealt with our struggles. He is *not* powerless.

4

While God handles so many of our struggles, we will still have some of those ongoing red dots in our lives. Does that mean God is no longer working on our struggles and has abandoned us? No. That is not at all consistent with scripture. In fact, I believe it is during those times that God does His very best work, fighting diligently for us.

***If God is really fighting for us in the midst of our struggles, why do you think we often fail to see it?***

## AUTHOR'S TOP 2

Here are two common reasons that I have run across:

1. We have become ________________.
2. We are too ______________ to the struggle.

Let's look at each of these.

5

**1. WE HAVE BECOME BITTER.** We discussed this in Step 3. When we have those false expectations that our lives should be free of suffering and struggles, then we will inevitably become bitter towards God. That bitterness will so darken our skies, that we can ______________ ourselves to how hard God is fighting for us. Don't let that happen. Bitterness leads to spiritual blindness.

> **BITTERNESS LEADS TO SPIRITUAL BLINDNESS.**

6 **2. WE ARE TOO CLOSE TO THE STRUGGLE.** Let's do a little experiment. Place your right hand out in front of your face as far away as possible. Come on, everyone must do it! Now, count the number of fingers you see. Next, take your right hand and place it right over your eyes and then count the number of fingers you see.

***What happened when you moved your hand over your eyes? Were you able to count the number of fingers?***

Okay, not the most elaborate experiment, but it makes the point. When something is too close, we can't __________ it clearly. In fact, when our hand was completely over our eyes, all we perceived was darkness. This is what happens when we become too close and consumed with our struggles—all we see is darkness.

This happened to me. All I could see was the disease. It was all-consuming. I became so focused on the illness, that I failed to see anything else. God was ______________ ________________________, but all I could see was darkness. I was just too close to the struggle.

I WAS JUST TOO CLOSE TO THE STRUGGLE.

***Have you ever had a struggle that was all-consuming? What did that feel like?***

Sometimes stepping back from the struggle requires us to change the way we ______________________. We must not allow ourselves to dwell on the problem. Admittedly, it is not an easy thing to do. But it is very necessary.

7

In order to step back, we first need to change the way we ____________ God and our struggles. I had an eye-opening experience with God that made a huge difference for me:

> One of my kids was going through a difficult situation in their life. I was thinking about the situation as I was praying to God. It broke my heart to see my kid suffer. And then it hit me. God is my Dad. God is the perfect Father in every way. And we are created in His Image. If I feel that way about my kids, how much more so does God feel that way towards me, His kid. It broke my heart to realize how much my suffering hurt Him. He was saying, *My child if you only knew the pain that your illness causes Me and how much it crushes Me to see all the suffering in this broken world.*
>
> I wept hard. I wept not for myself, but for my Dad who had to endure the suffering of His kid. I was reminded of Jesus when He saw the heart break of people who were grieving the death of Lazarus—and scripture tells us that our God *wept.* Indeed, God feels the heart break of His suffering kids more than we can possibly imagine.
>
> *When Skies Aren't Blue*, page 73

MY SUFFERING BROKE THE HEART OF GOD MORE THAN I COULD IMAGINE.

I finally had my eyes opened, realizing that my suffering broke the heart of God (my Heavenly Dad) more than I could imagine. My prayers changed. They were no longer a desperate plea to just take this disease from me. Instead, they became focused on my Father, who was suffering *with* me. I used to be so upset and just pray for all the things that I thought that He was *not* doing. But then I realized we were in this ________________, and I began to see all that He *was* doing (I document these in *When Skies Aren't Blue*). My prayers became those of sincere gratitude. But I had to step back from the struggle, and see things differently, to appreciate those amazing blessings.

***Despite your ongoing struggles, list the ways that God is still blessing your life.***

8 You might be in the middle of an unchangeable struggle right now and no longer *see* God at work.

***What are some things that you think you can do to help your "spiritual eyes" stay open?***

It is so important that we step back from our struggle and see the blessings from God. I wanted to share 3 key steps that have been personally helpful for me in my battle with this very difficult illness.

## AUTHOR'S 3 KEY STEPS

1. Know that your suffering ______________ God's heart.
2. Change the way you ____________.
3. Watch for the "just so _________________" moments.

Now, let's look at each of these steps in more detail.

9 **1. KNOW THAT YOUR SUFFERING BREAKS GOD'S HEART.** If you are right with God, then you are God's __________. He loves you more than you can know. If it crushes us to see our own child suffer, how much more so does it break the heart of God when we suffer? Now some may think that while it does break God's heart to watch us suffer, He does not truly ____________________ what we are going through.

***Does God understand our suffering and what it feels like on a personal level?***

We must never forget that while Jesus was fully God, He was also fully ________________. Jesus understands the suffering of the human condition because He went through it. He ______________ the deaths of those He loved. He felt the pain of estrangement from His own family, who ______________ Him. He knew the sting of ______________ from His closest friends, as they abandoned Him in His hour of need. And can you think of anyone more qualified to understand suffering than the One who endured the horror of ______________________? It is not a coincidence that God chose perhaps the most barbaric form of suffering to pay the price for our sins. Jesus suffered too. He understands our suffering on all levels.

You are *not* in this ___________. God understands all that you are going through on a very personal level. His heart breaks for your suffering. You are walking through this struggle together—Father and kid.

10

**2. CHANGE THE WAY YOU PRAY.** Step back from the struggle and see the big picture. Satan did this to you. And now you and your Heavenly Dad are suffering through this ____________________. Your prayers should not just be desperate pleas for complete and instant healing. Instead, they should become much more powerful, relational and deeper. At times they may even be tear filled, heartfelt, raw talks. Let Him know how much you hate that He (as your Dad) must endure this as well. Tell Him that you fully trust that He will walk you through this. Ask Him to ___________ your eyes and to *see* His blessings. And know that He will do that in miraculous and wonderful ways.

11

**3. WATCH FOR THE "JUST SO HAPPENED" MOMENTS.** Even if this red dot struggle (for now) remains, God is still doing amazing stuff. He is still blessing you. When you see those blessings pop up in your life, do *not* write them off as coincidence or "it just so happened".

**GOD IS THE GOD OF THOSE "JUST SO HAPPENED" MOMENTS.**

Write them down, record them and remember those "just so happened" moments. Let them strengthen your faith and relationship with your Heavenly Dad. And watch God light up your skies in the most unexpected ways.

**PROCEED WITH READING DR. ANDY'S TREATMENT PLAN ON PAGE 73.**

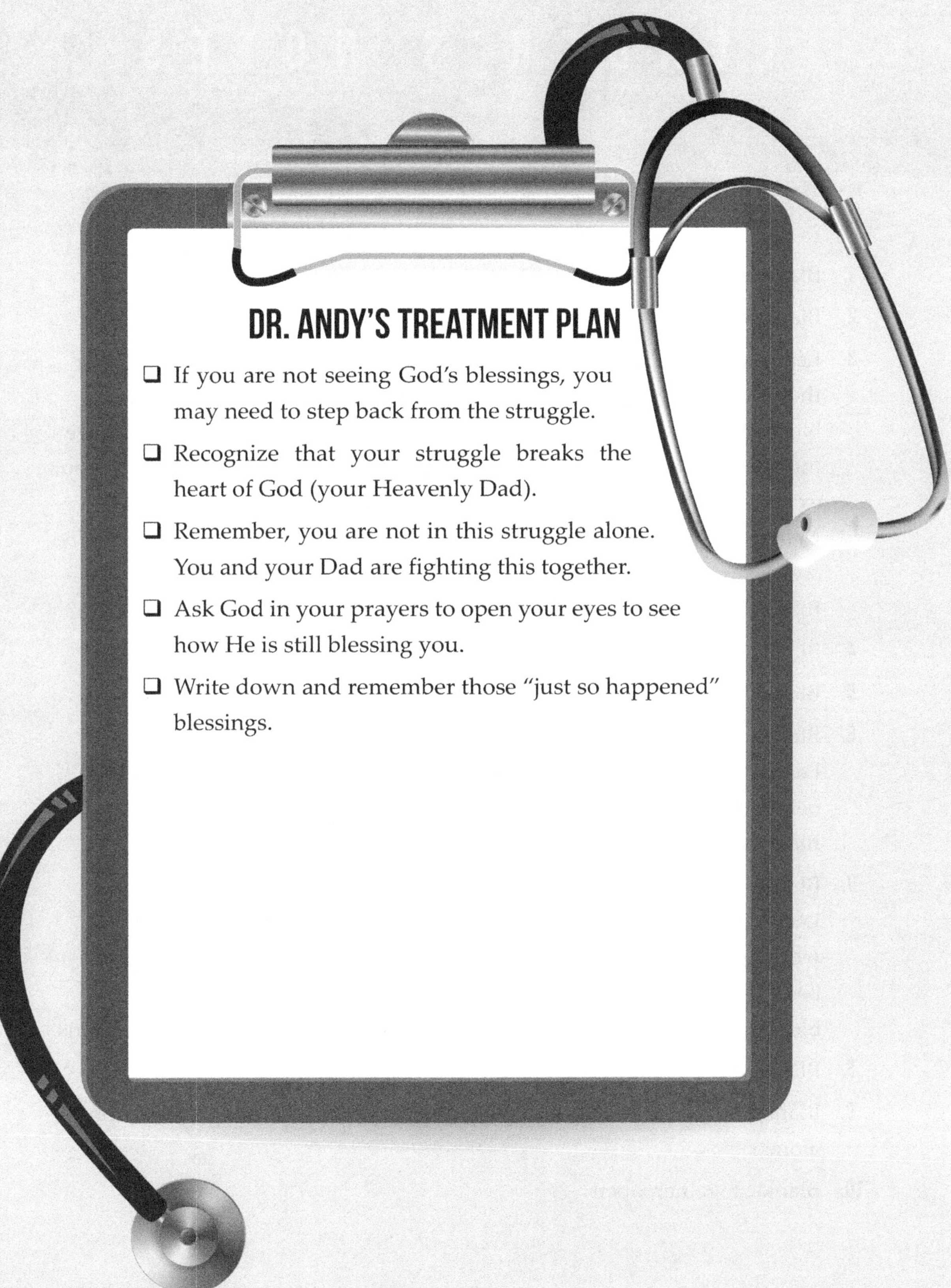

## DR. ANDY'S TREATMENT PLAN

- ☐ If you are not seeing God's blessings, you may need to step back from the struggle.
- ☐ Recognize that your struggle breaks the heart of God (your Heavenly Dad).
- ☐ Remember, you are not in this struggle alone. You and your Dad are fighting this together.
- ☐ Ask God in your prayers to open your eyes to see how He is still blessing you.
- ☐ Write down and remember those "just so happened" blessings.

# LEADER'S NOTES

1. Blank: extremes
2. Blanks: bitterness, darker, missing out
3. Leaders: Give your group plenty of time here. Have them first reflect on their lives and write down some of the struggles from their past. Then, have them write down the status of those struggles right now. Encourage them to share their answers with the group. If necessary, share one of your examples with the group to get them encouraged and sharing as well.
   *Note: The point here is that many of our problems get better or completely resolved over time as God is working in our lives.*
   Blanks: remembering, thanking
4. Blanks: bitter, close
5. Blank: blind
6. Blanks: see, still working
   Leaders: Encourage people to share. Recognizing the harm caused from being too close to the struggle is important.
   Blank: think
7. Blanks: view, together
   Leaders: Try to get the group to open up and share how God is still working in their lives. Opening up and verbalizing these blessings can be tremendously comforting and will help encourage others to see the blessings in their lives. These blessings can be *anything* good that happens.
8. Blanks: breaks, pray, happened
9. Blanks: kid, understand, human, grieved, rejected, betrayal, crucifixion, alone
10. Blanks: together, open

STEP 8

# *Battle That God Amnesia*

*God handled this in the past, and He will do so in the future.*

# GROUP DISCUSSION

Welcome to Step 8. Get ready to take hold of a powerful spiritual tool. If used correctly, it can bring you peace and comfort, even in the middle of some of the roughest storms in life. Let's begin with prayer (You can use the one below as a guide).

> *Father, thank You for caring so much for us. We know we tend to forget those times that You have stepped into our lives and handled our struggles. We ask that You help us to better remember all that You have done in our lives. And for us to find comfort from that. In Jesus Name, Amen.*

(Answers to blanks found on page 82.)

**1**

In *When Skies Aren't Blue*, I talked about the "God Amnesia Syndrome". Of course, the physician side of me must make *everything* a disease or syndrome.

***What is the "God Amnesia Syndrome"?***

The "God Amnesia Syndrome" is that tendency to ________________ the amazing things that God has done in and through our lives. Unfortunately, our brains are wired in such a way that we tend to forget things.

**2** In Step 7, we talked about those barriers that get in the way of our truly *seeing* God at work in our lives. But even if we put those critical things in place, and we do see God at work, we run into another problem. And that is, let some time go by, and we may develop the "God Amnesia Syndrome".

***What are the spiritual dangers of the "God Amnesia Syndrome"?***

The syndrome of forgetting the ways that God has blessed us in the *past* can cause harm to our *current* relationship with God. We can end up not being thankful for all the good He does in our lives. In addition, the "God Amnesia Syndrome" can easily send us into a cycle of ______________.

***What is the major problem that develops following Step 7 in the cycle of worry?***

Because we have ____________________ how God has stepped in and handled our past problems, we end up subjecting ourselves to that cycle of worry all over again. How powerful would it be to recognize that God has brought us through a similar situation in the past? And then, we can have confidence that He will do so _____________. No need to worry.

> GOD'S GOT THIS, ALWAYS HAS AND ALWAYS WILL.

In my own health struggles, I frequently find myself struggling with recurrent symptoms. Some of them are quite alarming, especially those related to my cardiovascular system and heart rhythms. When these scary symptoms occur, my initial reaction is to go into that cycle of worry once again. But then I take a deep breath and remember that God has brought me through similar symptoms in the past. Based on that, I have confidence that He will do it again. God's got this, always has and always will.

**3**

"Remembering what God has done in the past is the key to keeping peace and confidence during future storms in life."

*When Skies Aren't Blue*, page 87

***What are some of the struggles that God has handled in your past?***

God may have handled some health problems that were so painful for you at the time. God may have walked you through a scary financial situation. God may have helped you through a traumatic family, marital or relational situation. It all seemed so overwhelming at the time, but He brought you through it.

If a problem develops, you know He'll take you through it ______________. Indeed, remembering what God has done in the past is the key to keeping *peace* and *confidence* during ______________ storms in life.

4 But we have a problem. We need to ______________________ the amazing things that God has done for us in the *past* to give us confidence for *future* struggles. Unfortunately, we have a tendency to ______________. God knows we all have a tendency to forget. So, He gives us the solution.

Let's look at a fascinating story from the book of Joshua to see what God's solution is to the "God Amnesia Syndrome". Some quick background to the story: God had just done some miraculous things, such as parting the Jordan river, so that His people could safely pass into the promised land. God was concerned that His people would eventually forget what He had done. So, He tells them to do something interesting (read about that in Joshua 4:1-7).

***What does God tell His people to do?***

***Why did He tell them to do that?***

God told them to put down a __________ _____ __________ taken from the Jordan riverbed. The idea is that every time someone passed by this area, they would see the pile of rocks, and it would serve as a ______________________ of the miraculous thing that God had done. It would also be a great source of ____________________. They would see these stones and be reminded that God handled their *past* struggles. This would give them ______________________ for those *future* storms in life as well. *Great idea God!*

DEVELOP YOUR OWN PILE OF ROCKS.

**5** Let's talk about developing our own pile of rocks.

***When God steps in and does these amazing things for us, what are some ways that we can go about recording them?***

We could all throw down a bunch of rocks in the middle of our living rooms, but that might be a bit of a tripping hazard. I'm sure you came up with some great ideas. Here is my top 5 list:

## AUTHOR'S TOP 5 LIST

1. Keep a written ________________, a "God diary" of all those times God has come through.
2. Record it on your ________________. You can use an app like "Notes".
3. Keep a journal on your ________________________.
4. Leave ________________ ____________ reminders.
5. Record it on a ______________________ on the date that God came through.

*Author's Note*

*We are wired differently when it comes to remembering things. Find the way(s) that work best for you.*

**6** I tend to use my phone, since it is so accessible. When something happens where God comes through, I can very easily dictate it into the Notes app on my phone. But I also like to use the old school sticky note route. In *When Skies Aren't Blue,* I shared with you a story where God stepped in and healed a dangerous heart rhythm. The timing was truly miraculous with how it all played out. I encourage you to go back and read that story. The miraculous healing happened at precisely 9:46 AM. When I got home from the hospital, I put a sticky note in my room which simply reads, "9:46". So, every day when I get dressed, I see it.

*Reminder note in my room*

My heart still does periodically go into those scary heart rhythms. But instead of panicking, I see this note. Then I calmly remind myself that God handled this in the past, and He can do so in the future. __________ __________ pile of rocks can be that comforting.

**7** There is so much that happens in our day-to-day lives. This brings up a fair question:

***What types of things should you record in your own pile of rocks?***

We will occasionally have those "wow" moments, those times where God comes through in an obvious and miraculous way. Of course, those "wow" moments should be recorded. But often, God works in more _______________ ways. We may have had a problem which resolved and think, "Well *that* issue worked out well." Record those seemingly simple "just so happened" moments too. They are not coincidence. Record your __________________ prayers (big ones and little ones). Record it all.

**RECORD THOSE JUST SO HAPPENED MOMENTS**

**8** If you have not already done so, I want to encourage you to start your own pile of rocks today. Be diligent and stay __________________. God is always working. When (not if) the next struggle comes your way, take out your pile of rocks and read it. Remind yourself of how much God has worked in your life. I think you will be pleasantly surprised at the power and comfort this will bring you during those current and future storms.

***When God comes through for you, how will you record it?***

**PROCEED WITH READING DR. ANDY'S TREATMENT PLAN ON PAGE 83.**

# LEADER'S NOTES

1. Blank: forget
2. Blanks: worry, forgotten, again
3. Leaders: Challenge your group to really think through this. Really encourage discussion. Use your own examples to get the group talking. Remembering these things will serve as a tremendous source of comfort for those future storms in life.
   Blanks: again, future
4. Blanks: remember, forget, pile of rocks, reminder, comfort, confidence
5. Blanks: journal, phone, computer, sticky note, calendar
6. Blanks: Your own
7. Blanks: subtle, answered
8. Blank: current
   Leaders: Encourage them to list their favorite method here (i.e. phone, computer, sticky note, calendar, journal, etc.).

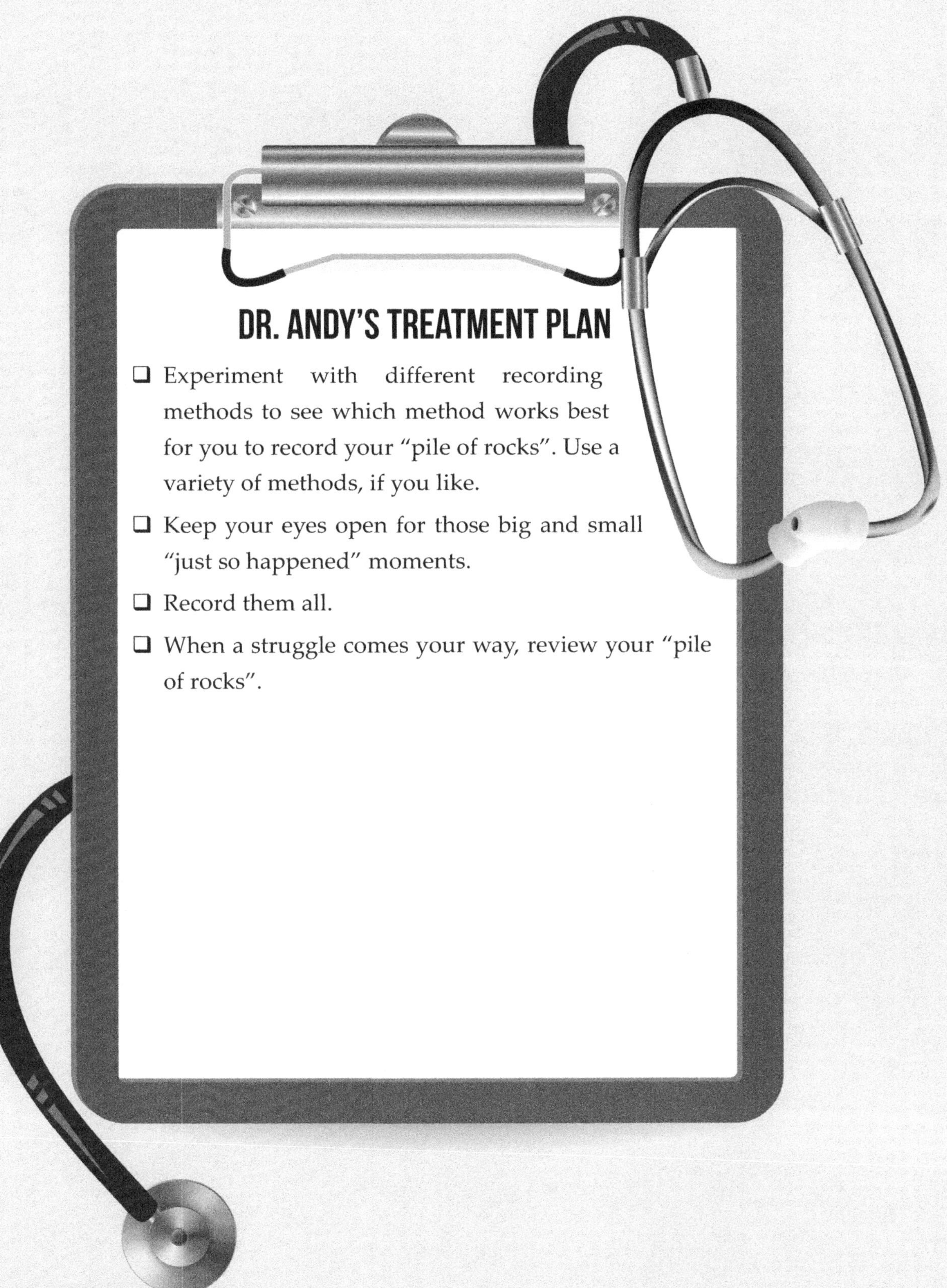

## DR. ANDY'S TREATMENT PLAN

- ❑ Experiment with different recording methods to see which method works best for you to record your "pile of rocks". Use a variety of methods, if you like.
- ❑ Keep your eyes open for those big and small "just so happened" moments.
- ❑ Record them all.
- ❑ When a struggle comes your way, review your "pile of rocks".

STEP 9

# *Dwell On The Green Dots*

*We can have that peace which transcends all understanding.*

# GROUP DISCUSSION

**START HERE** In Step 9, we are going to learn to train our minds so that we can have blue skies, even in the darkest of times. Let's get started with prayer (you can use the one below as a guide).

*Father, I know my life is polka dotted with both the good and the bad. Help me to learn to dwell on those wonderful green dot blessings from You. And help me to resist focusing on those scary what ifs in life. Thank you for being the God who is near, regardless of what the enemy throws my way. In Jesus Name, Amen.*

(Answers to blanks found on page 92.)

**1** Let's review an important concept we discussed back in Step 3 from James 1:2, "Consider it pure joy, my brothers and sisters, whenever you face trials of many kinds."

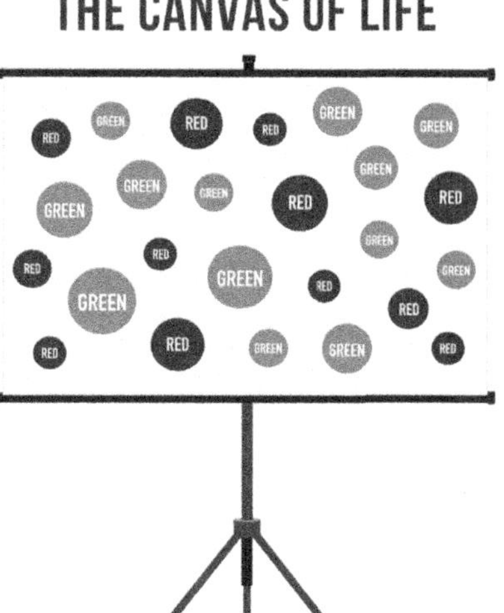


The canvas of life illustration is based on James telling us that our lives would have these trials of "many kinds". If you recall, the English translation for "many kinds" is: _______________ _________.

***What do the red dots represent?***

***What do the green dots represent?***

***What are some of those red and green dots in your life?***

The red dots represent the ________ things in our lives. These could be physical and mental health issues, financial struggles, relationship/family problems, job issues, grieving the loss of a loved one, etc.

The green dots represent the ____________ things in our lives. These are the blessings from God. These could be friends, family, spouse, a beloved pet, a great church, financial/job stability, stable health, etc.

**2** Keep this concept of the red and green dots in mind as we study a set of verses written by the Apostle Paul. Paul wrote these words when he was in prison for his faith. His freedom was gone and his skies were as dark as could be (read Philippians 4:4-8).

***How does it change things for you knowing that Paul was in prison when he wrote these words?***

Paul did not have an ____________________ view of the world. He knew that life gets hard at times. He understood in a very personal way that we will all face difficult struggles. And the fact that he was in such a struggle when he wrote these words, gives it so much more power. It makes it real.

**3** Paul said that we can have a peace that *transcends all understanding.*

***What do you think that means?***

We can have peace when logically we should not. In the darkest and scariest of times, when others would be riddled with fear and ____________________, we can have real, God-empowered ________________.

Paul is teaching us that no matter what our circumstances may be, how scary they may feel, or how dark our skies may appear, we can have that peace which *transcends all understanding*.

4 Paul tells us the key to having that amazing peace is *what* we allow our minds to ______________ on. Paul is basically saying that a key to getting this peace which *transcends all understanding* is choosing to *dwell* on the ______________ dots, *not* the ___________ dots. It seems so easy, right? And yet it is not.

***When we are in a struggle, why is it so hard to focus on the green dots?***

***Why is thinking about the red dots so natural?***

Here is the bottom line: it is just human nature. We naturally dwell on those scary "what ifs" in life.

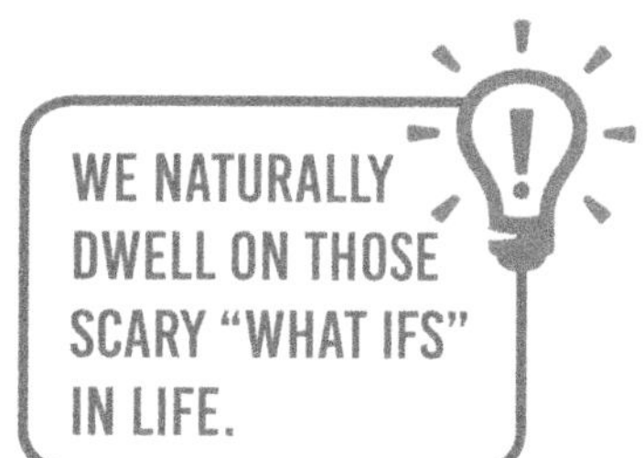


5 This is something that I must deal with. Due to the nature of this autonomic disease, I regularly face some scary symptoms. And then the "what ifs" follow. *What if* this nausea gets worse, and I can no longer eat? *What if* my blood pressure keeps dropping, and I lose consciousness? *What if* this heart rhythm gets worse, and I end up needing cardiac defibrillation? *What if, what if, what if.* We are all so drawn to dwelling on those "what ifs" in life.

***What are some of the scary "what ifs" you tend to worry about?***

6 What we choose to dwell on will impact our lives on many levels. And we have a very real enemy, Satan, who is working against us. Look at the diagram below.

***What do you think Satan wants you to dwell on and why?***

Satan knows that if he can get you to stay focused on the red dots, then your mind will be consumed with those worrisome "what ifs" in life. He knows in time that will incapacitate you with stress, fear and anxiety. These will lead to darker skies, and that is where he wants you. The last thing the enemy wants you to do is cling to God and focus on Him and His ____________________ (read 2 Corinthians 10:3-5).

***According to these verses, where is one key area that spiritual warfare takes place?***

WHAT WE CHOOSE TO DWELL ON IS A SPIRITUAL BATTLE.

These verses tell us that spiritual warfare is a battle for our ___________. God says that we are to take our *thoughts* captive to obey Him. We must choose to focus on and be thankful for the green dots. God says we need to actively reject thinking on and worrying about the "what ifs" of the red dots. This is taking the fight to the enemy. Never forget: *what* we choose to dwell on is a ______________________ battle.

**7** We will all have different green dots as God has blessed us in unique ways. But, if you are right with God (see "How To Get Right With God" at whenskiesarentblue.com), then we all share one common green dot. And this is the biggest green dot of all. It is the green dot that should dominate our canvas of life. Paul tells us very clearly what that wonderful green dot is with four very powerful words: "The Lord is ____________!"

So, let's all make an important addition to our Canvas Of Life right now. Fill in your name at the top and then next to the green dot, the biggest green dot blessing of all, write: "The Lord is near!"

**_______________'S CANVAS OF LIFE**

GREEN ______________________________

*Author's Note*

*You can find and print out copies of "The Canvas of Life" at whenskiesarentblue.com.*

8 Paul challenges us to keep our thoughts on the biggest green dot blessing of all: "The Lord is near!"

***Why do you think this green dot is the most important one to dwell on?***

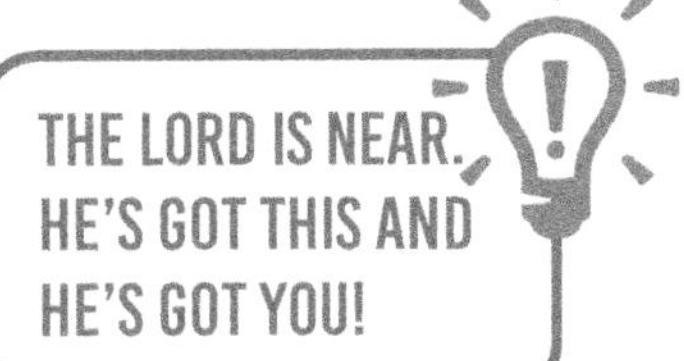


This ultimate green dot is the antidote (yes, another doctor word) to ____________ possible scary "what if". If you are facing a scary health struggle, no worries . . . "The Lord is near" . . . He's got this. If you are dealing with an overwhelming financial crisis, no worries . . . "The Lord is near". . . He's got this. If you are in a painful family/marital/relational situation, no worries . . . "The Lord is near". . . He's got this. Whatever it is you are facing . . . "The Lord is near". . . He's got this, and He's got you! Stay focused on the most powerful green dot.

Author's Note

*Often people with chronic illness feel a sense of loneliness. Even if they are blessed with loving friends and family, they feel emotionally alone because it seems no one truly understands what they are going through and feeling. Remember, God fully understands suffering, and His heart breaks with you and for you. You are not alone. He is near.*

9 So, we have a ______________ in the midst of our struggles. We can choose to focus on the worrisome "what ifs", but then we will be consumed with anxiety and dark skies. Or we can choose to focus on the blessings of an amazing God, *who is near.* He will take us through the struggle. He always has and always will. Dwelling on that will bring us a peace that *transcends all understanding* and will then brighten even the darkest of skies.

**PROCEED WITH READING DR. ANDY'S TREATMENT PLAN ON PAGE 93.**

# LEADER'S NOTES

1. Blanks: polka dots, bad, good
2. Blank: unrealistic
3. Blanks: anxiety, peace
4. Blanks: dwell, green, red
5. Leaders: This is pretty personal and people may feel reluctant to share. Obviously, give them the choice to share or not, but you can start the discussion by mentioning some of the scary "what ifs" in your life.
6. Blanks: blessings, minds, spiritual
7. Blank: near

   Leaders: People can fill out the sample canvas (only the top is shown) on the page with their name and fill in the blank next to the "Green" dot with "The Lord is near". Encourage them to fill out their personal printed out copy as well at another time. Additional copies of "The Canvas of Life" are available to print at whenskiesarentblue.com.
8. Blank: every
9. Blank: choice

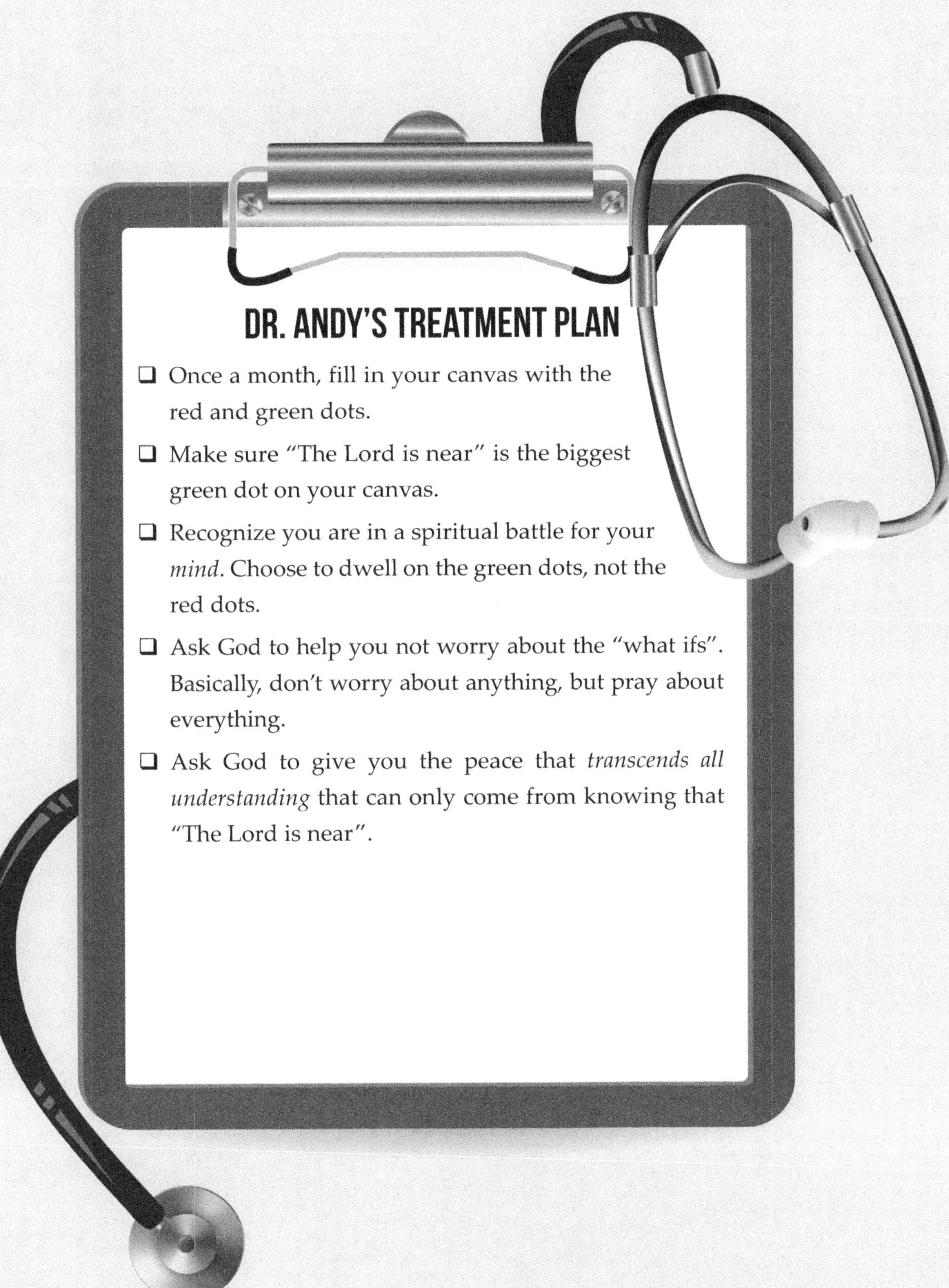

## DR. ANDY'S TREATMENT PLAN

- ❑ Once a month, fill in your canvas with the red and green dots.
- ❑ Make sure "The Lord is near" is the biggest green dot on your canvas.
- ❑ Recognize you are in a spiritual battle for your *mind*. Choose to dwell on the green dots, not the red dots.
- ❑ Ask God to help you not worry about the "what ifs". Basically, don't worry about anything, but pray about everything.
- ❑ Ask God to give you the peace that *transcends all understanding* that can only come from knowing that "The Lord is near".

STEP 10

# *Remember One Day The Skies Will Be Eternally Blue*

*Our current struggles are but a tiny blip in time.*

# GROUP DISCUSSION

Congratulations! You have reached the final Step. Get ready to take hold of a lasting hope that will overcome even the darkest of skies. Let's start with prayer (you can use the one below as a guide).

*Father, help us to understand that this world is not our final home. And that while some of our current struggles may seem unchangeable, they are still temporary. We know that You will make everything perfect, forever. Through this lesson help us to find comfort and strength from Your promise of a perfect eternity. In Jesus Name, Amen.*

(Answers to blanks found on page 104.)

## 1

I remember so well the sadness and heavy emotions when I realized that my illness was not going away. It was painful on many levels knowing that I was going to be sick for the rest of my life. This was going to be an unchangeable struggle.

***What are some of those unchangeable struggles we may face in life?***

We all face those ______________________ struggles in life. Some of those things may be: physical or mental health issues, death of a loved one, financial calamity, divorce, estrangement from a family member or close friend and more.

When we realize those struggles are unchangeable and we are going to have them for the rest of our lives, it can so easily lead to the loss of ______________. The absence of hope is _______________ and despair can take an already dark sky and turn it ____________.

2 Where do we find hope when we know that our struggles are not going away? Where do we find hope when we realize that we are going to live with this for the rest of our lives? The answer is found in ____________ ________________________.

Let's take a look at some promises from God. As we do ask yourself, "What is the perspective God wants me to have?" Read Matthew 6:19-20, 1 Corinthians 15:50 and 2 Corinthians 4:18.

***How do you think God wants you to view this world?***

God is making it clear that this world is ________________________. He wants us to understand that this world is not our final home.

***Why would we naturally tend to view this world as our final home?***

This world is all that we know, all that we can see and all that we experience. So, it is understandable that we would naturally think this is it. That is why God challenges us to __________________ differently. Remember, spiritual warfare is a battle for our ______________. It is a battle for how we think. God says we must see our world through different eyes—know that it is temporary and know it is *not* our final home.

3 At the very end of the Bible, God gives us a glimpse of our final home (read Revelation 21:1-4).

***How does God describe our final home?***

In our final home, God will dwell with us. He will wipe away every _________ (it will be pure joy). There will be no _____________ (this home will be permanent). There will be no mourning, crying or pain. The unchangeable struggles will be ___________, forever. It will be perfect, beyond anything we can comprehend.

Author's Note

*These promises are not just a fairy tale wish to help us cope. We can prove the Bible is true. We know for a fact that our final home is just as real as the world we currently live in. If you want those facts, and a powerful faith builder, please look at the "Facts Behind The Faith" seminar at whenskiesarentblue.com.*

4 Tapping into this eternal hope of our final home can be very comforting, regardless of what your unchangeable struggle may be.

***Look at the list of unchangeable struggles you listed under #1 (page 96) in this session. What will happen to these things in your final home?***

Physical health problems will no longer be an issue; our new bodies will be _________________ in every possible way. Emotional and psychological struggles will be replaced with the perfect ___________ of God. We will never grieve the loss of a loved one; death will be no longer. The pain from broken marriages and failed family relationships will be eternally replaced with the most incredible and wonderful relationship of all—we will dwell with our __________________. The unchangeable struggles of this temporary world will no longer exist.

5 For those of you who are suffering from chronic health issues, I would like to give you a passage that has been helpful for me. In fact, I have it regularly pop up on my phone as a constant reminder and source of comfort (read 2 Corinthians 4:16).

***How do you think God wants you to view your current body?***

God is telling us that the ___________ ________ is *not* your current body, which is decaying (sick, suffering or struggling). The real you is ________________. The real you is healthy, strong and beautiful and made in the image of the Creator. The real you is not winding down in sickness and weakness. Instead, it is getting stronger, as that amazing day approaches, when the real you will be with your Creator in perfection, forever.

**WHEN YOUR BODY IS SUFFERING, REMIND YOURSELF THAT IT IS NOT THE REAL YOU.**

6 Some may say that viewing this world as temporary, and not our final home, is a fatalistic view of life.

***Is this true? Does focusing on our final home mean we do not value our current life? Does this mean we are desiring our own death?***

Understanding that this world is temporary is actually a ________________ way to approach life. We can be grateful for the ____________ things that we have, but we do not need to desperately cling to them because we know they are temporary. And for the _________ things that we deal with, we can endure them because we know they are also temporary. There is a huge difference between cherishing the day when God will finally make everything perfect, and somehow desiring our own death.

Let's take a look at a helpful passage in scripture to understand how we should view this life (read Philippians 1:21).

***What did the Apostle Paul have to say about this issue?***

Paul made it clear that __________________ will far surpass anything we can imagine in this world, and he is looking forward to someday being there (to die is gain). But in the meantime, he wanted to make a difference for Jesus in this ____________ (to live is Christ).

I get that. I suffer. There is a part of me that longs for that wonderful day when I will be healthy and perfect forever. Yet, I still cherish the gift of life that God gave me. I want to make the most of it, and to impact my world for Christ while I am here. That is a big reason why I wrote *When Skies Aren't Blue.*

***How can you use your suffering to make a difference for Jesus (to live is Christ)?***

Suffering is so common in our world. Christians and non-Christians suffer. Can you imagine the ______________________ of living with these awful struggles without God? How would it feel to truly believe that my one and only life is now destroyed because of this ongoing struggle? There would be no ___________. That is the futility of life, if this world with all the suffering is our final home.

What a huge opportunity this presents. You can show them the ______________ that prove God and the Bible. You can prove to them that this is not their final home. Give them that hope. They crave it; they need it.

> *Author's Note*
>
> *Sometimes it can be intimidating to talk with someone about God, or we may not know exactly what to say. An easy way to make that difference is to direct them to the website: whenskiesarentblue.com. The resources they need to find that hope in the midst of their suffering can be found there.*

8 One of the illustrations that has been helpful for me through this illness has been the eternal tape measure.

**ETERNAL TAPE MEASURE**

***How is this tape measure an accurate view of "life"? How can this help us cope with our struggles?***

The tape measure represents your life on earth and your life eternal.

**ETERNAL TAPE MEASURE**

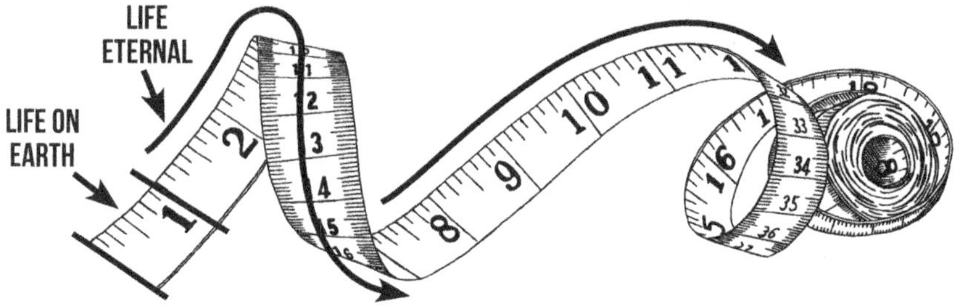

LIFE ETERNAL

LIFE ON EARTH

The __________ ______________ is your life in this body in this world. Everything (the good and the bad) happens in that first inch. Then you die, and you move into your final home, in your perfect body, in paradise. And that goes on and on and on. That is very much the Biblical way God wants you to view life.

Now let's apply that view to whatever your unchangeable struggles may be. The unchangeable struggles become minuscule. In fact, in the big picture of your entire life (whole tape measure), it hardly registers. We tend to think *this* life and *these* bodies are everything. But when we put our suffering into the eternal tape measure, we realize it is just a small ______________ in time. It is *not even an unchangeable.* It may be in this world, but this world is just a blip. It is not our final home. This perspective can bring about a powerful peace and comfort regardless of what our earthly struggle may be.

**9** In John 14, Jesus was telling His disciples about that final home. They no doubt heard some amazing things, and of course asked the obvious question, "What is the way to get to this home?" Jesus responded with these incredible words . . . (read John 14:6).

IT IS ONLY THROUGH JESUS THAT WE CAN BE IN OUR FINAL HOME—WHERE OUR SKIES WILL BE FOREVER BLUE.

PROCEED WITH READING DR. ANDY'S TREATMENT PLAN ON PAGE 103.

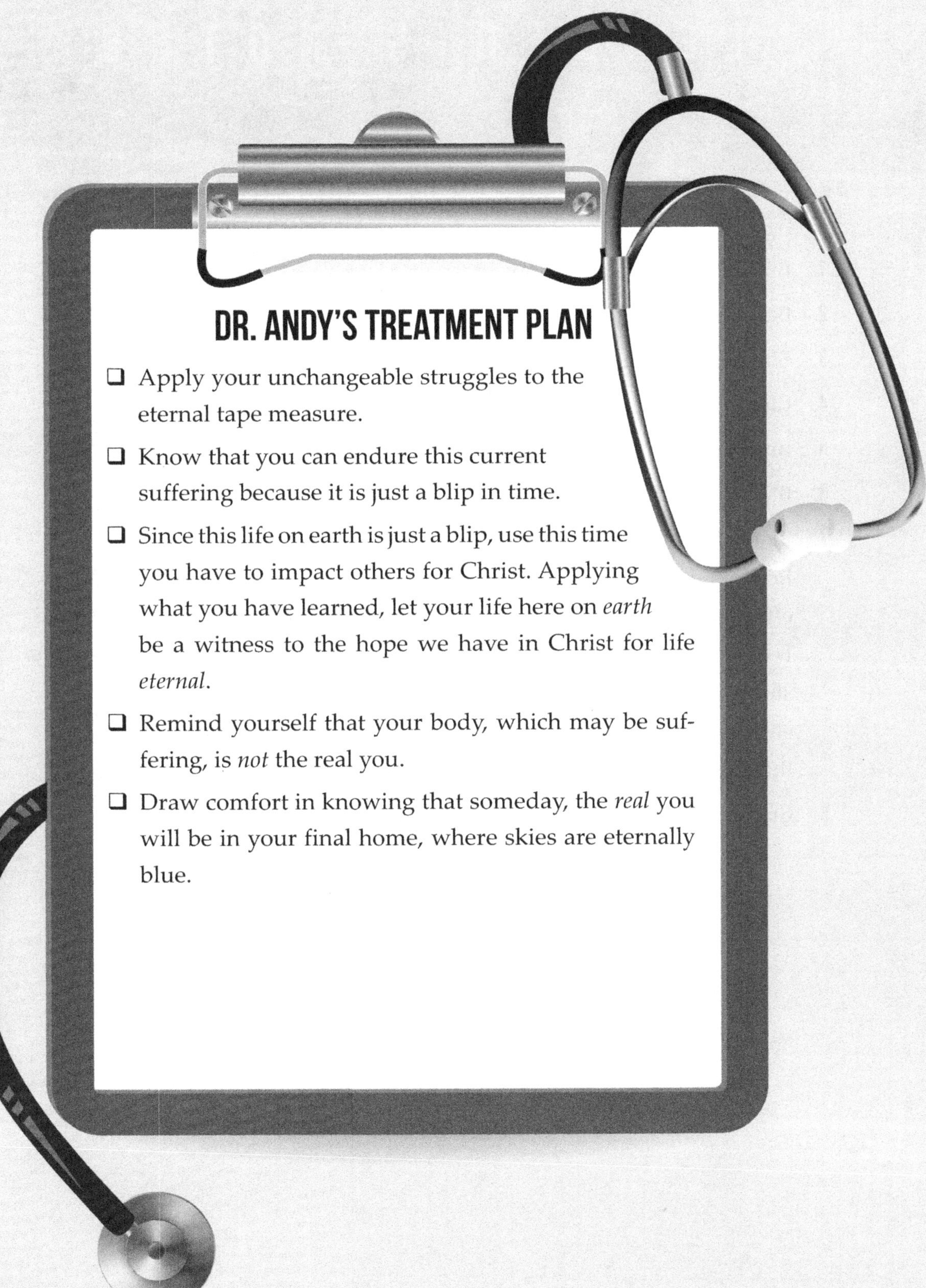

# DR. ANDY'S TREATMENT PLAN

- ❑ Apply your unchangeable struggles to the eternal tape measure.
- ❑ Know that you can endure this current suffering because it is just a blip in time.
- ❑ Since this life on earth is just a blip, use this time you have to impact others for Christ. Applying what you have learned, let your life here on *earth* be a witness to the hope we have in Christ for life *eternal*.
- ❑ Remind yourself that your body, which may be suffering, is *not* the real you.
- ❑ Draw comfort in knowing that someday, the *real* you will be in your final home, where skies are eternally blue.

# LEADER'S NOTES

1. Blanks: unchangeable, hope, despair, black
2. Blanks: God's promises, temporary, think, minds
3. Blanks: tear, death, gone
4. Blanks: perfect, peace, Creator
5. Blanks: real you, internal
6. Blanks: healthy, good, bad
7. Blanks: Heaven, world, hopelessness, hope, facts
   Leaders: This is a great opportunity for those in the group to talk about effective ways that they can use their suffering to help others.
   For example, as they apply the principles they have learned through this study guide to their lives, others can see how they are dealing with the suffering effectively and then they can point them to the ultimate hope they have in a relationship with Christ.
8. Blanks: first inch, blip

# RESOURCES

For the resources mentioned in this book,
check out the author's website:
whenskiesarentblue.com

*When Skies Aren't Blue*
book by Andy Laurie, MD

"How To Get Right With God"
handout

"Facts Behind The Faith"
free video seminar

"Why Bad Things Happen To Good People"
free video seminar

"Creation vs. Evolution"
free video seminar

"Canvas of Life"
worksheet

# ABOUT THE AUTHORS

*Andy with his wife Cyndi*

Andy Laurie, MD is the author of the Amazon bestseller, *When Skies Aren't Blue.* Dr. Laurie practiced emergency radiology for nearly thirty years before illness caused him to retire. In addition, he has been a pastor at The Bridge Christian Church in Tucson, Arizona, for 25 years. He has courageously battled a serious disease of the autonomic nervous system for over two decades. Dr. Laurie and his wife, Cyndi, were married in 1991 after he graduated from medical school. They have four grown children, two grandchildren and make their home in Tucson with their beloved dogs.

Nicole Baron has been a professional graphic designer for 22 years, specializing in book design for the last 20 years. She has also been a minister at The Bridge Christian Church for 12 years where she has been working with Dr. Laurie. Nicole was married to Chet Baron in 2004. They have an adult son and adopted daughter and live in Tucson, Arizona.

Made in United States
North Haven, CT
21 February 2024

49024030R00063